CATCH THE VISION

© 2010 The Order of Saint Anne—Bethany

25 Hillside Avenue,
Arlington, MA 02476–5818

All rights reserved. Except for brief quotations in critical articles or reviews,
no part of this book may be reproduced in any manner whatsoever
without the prior permission, in writing, of The Order of Saint Anne-Bethany.

A cataloguing-in-publication record for this book is available
from the Library of Congress.

Design by Claire MacMaster, barefoot art graphic design
deepwater-creative.com

Printed in China through Printworks Int. Ltd

ISBN 978-0-615-31263-7

CATCH THE VISION

*Celebrating a Century of the
Order of Saint Anne*

edited by

Charles Hefling
with
Sister Ana Clara, OSA
Erica Gelser
Mary Meader
Sister Olga, OSA
Julia Slayton

Published by The Order of Saint Anne—Bethany
Arlington, Massachusetts
2010

Catch the vision.

Hold it in trust.

Preserve it.

Carry it on.

You have always to be looking further,
opening doors and going through them.
All before was but a preparation
for something further.

Henry Lucius Moultrie Cary, SSJE

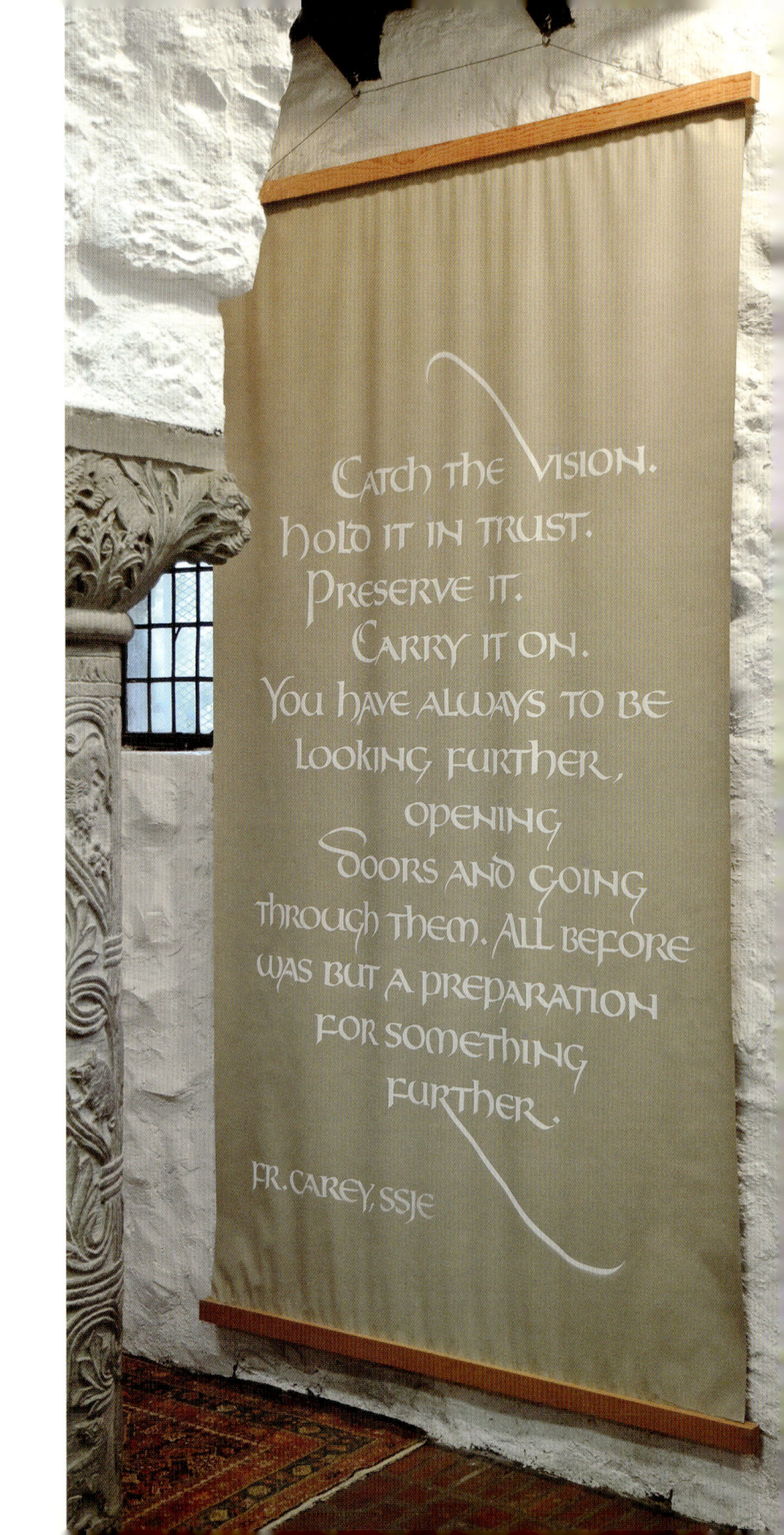

To
the memory of

MOTHER ETHELDRED, OSA
Foundress and first Mother Superior of the
Order of Saint Anne

and in thanksgiving for the faithful ministry of

SISTER ANA CLARA, OSA
Superior of the Bethany Convent
since 1992

this book is affectionately dedicated.

Contents

    Preface
    Desmond Tutu   9

    Foreword
    M. Thomas Shaw, SSJE   11

    Welcome
    Sister Ana Clara, OSA   13

1   **Mother Etheldred and 'The Small House at Arlington'**   15
    Interlude: *A Place with Welcome at Its Heart*
    Margaret Guenther   21

2   **The St Anne's School**   23
    Interlude: *Lives Knit Together*
    Cheryl Cronin   25

3   **Children**   27
    Interlude: *Where Your Treasure Is*
    Jacqueline Haslett   30

4   **The Religious Life in Anglicanism**   33

5   **Habits**   39
    Interlude: *A Chorus of Women's Voices*
    Sheryl Kujawa-Holbrook   40

6   **The Father Founder**   43
    Interlude: *Abundant, Gracious Hospirality*
    Barbara C. Harris   47

7   **From Temple Street to Harvard Square**   49
    Interlude: *Nothing Showy*
    Erica Gelser   54
    Interlude: *Coming Home*
    Eleanor Panasevich   55

8	Foxborough	57
	Interlude: *A Sweet Bond of Love* Curtis Almquist, SSJE	59
9	St Anne's Chapel	61
	Interlude: *A Different Kind of Space* Andrew McGowan	65
10	England, the Fourth Foundation	67
11	China	71
12	The Philippines	77
	Interlude: *Remembering Upi* Constancio Manguramas	81
13	Mission Far and Wide	83
14	Chicago	87
	Interlude: *Bethany Thanksgivings* Mark Hollingsworth, Jr.	89
15	Bethany: Lincoln and Arlington	91
	Interlude: *Seasons of Love* Tansy Chapman	98
	Postlude: *Reading the Word* Julia Slayton	101
	Envoi: *There's So Much More* Sister Olga, OSA	103
	Thank You *Acknowledgments* *Sources* *Picture Credits*	105
	Houses of the Order of Saint Anne 1910–2010	110

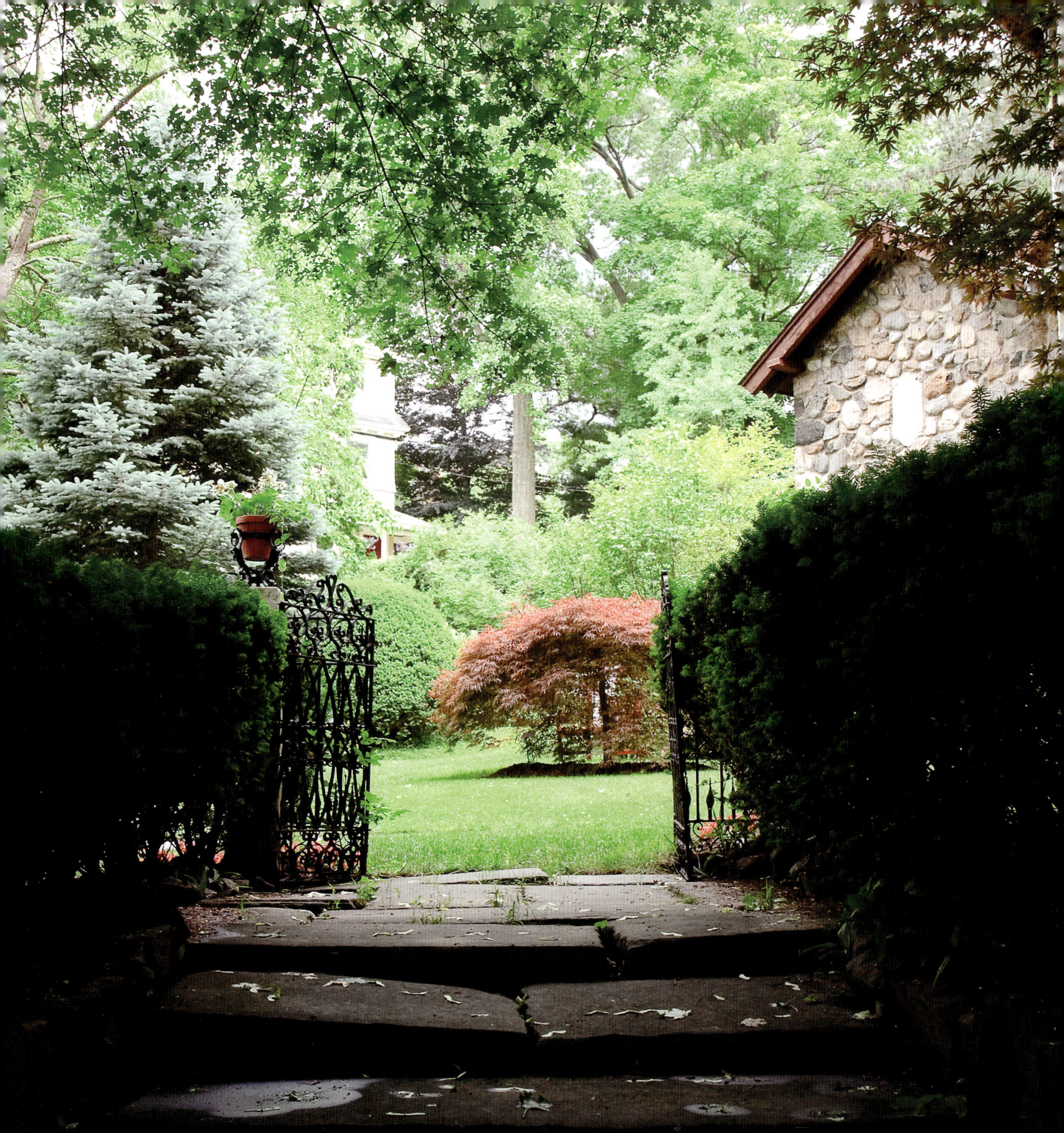

Preface

The peace meets you at the garden gate. There is a particular odor to a place that has been prayed in. It clings to the walls of old churches and seeps into the wood like oil. At Bethany every leaf and tree, every stone and flower seems to be infused with the prayers of the faithful. People have prayed here. Now, after a hundred years, a small band of people so transparently holy, serene, and yes, joyous—even somewhat mischievous, with a twinkle in their eyes—hold open the spaciousness of the holy for people of every faith who come here to pray.

I first came to Bethany in 2002, driving from my temporary home in Cambridge for the Wednesday morning Eucharist at the convent. After the Eucharistic feast we would gather for breakfast, a motley group enjoying the warm, easy hospitality of the Sisters of the Order of Saint Anne. I also came for monthly quiet days to this wonderful place that exudes so much serenity. In the years since, I have enjoyed the assurance of their prayers and the memory of their joy-filled faith.

Through the years the Sisters of the Order of Saint Anne have traveled around the world and across the street to offer their ministry of hospitality, pastoral care, and prayer with grace. Now, as they look forward to a second century of witness in the world I invite you to join me in joyful thanksgiving and prayer for their work.

God be praised for these God's faithful servants. When we get to heaven (those of us who do), we will be amazed to learn what we who are so busy in the world owe to them.

✠ Desmond Tutu
Archbishop of Cape Town, *retired*

Bishop Tutu at breakfast in the Bethany convent, with Sisters Olga, Maria Teresa, Judith, Ana Clara, Maria Agnes, and Felicitas.

CORPUS CHRISTI SALVA ME

Foreword

The Sisters of Saint Anne have been my friends for more than thirty years. During that time, I have conducted retreats for them, done workshops, been their chaplain, celebrated the Eucharist with them, and preached to them; and for the past fifteen years, I have been their Bishop Visitor. I like to say that, during all those years of friendship and collaboration, they haven't done a single thing I have told them to do.

Countless times, with the best intentions, I have listened, reflected back, shared visions, and thought we had come to a common understanding—only to discover at a later date that they had decided to follow a completely different track. I have thrown up my hands in despair at what I thought was a waste of my time. I have lost a significant amount of hair in frustration as they changed their mind yet again. I have been caught up in an inner fury at what I have perceived as their stalling tactics.

And you know what? They have, in the end, almost always been right. These warm, loving, seemingly agreeable women, because of their prayer and their gift of self-awareness, have an unswerving compass that takes them directly to God's will for them even when it has meant embracing change or starting again, in a new place or a new way. Especially in these later years, their gift of hospitality and collaboration, their faithfulness in worship in a world that is too busy, too harsh, and too judgmental have been a haven and a place of nurture for hundreds of us.

'Sometimes we see, sometimes we don't,' I have heard them say; 'but our Lord walks beside us and our aim is to always go on, laying down and taking up as the Holy Spirit leads us.'

By their abiding example, we have been and are blessed.

☩ M. Thomas Shaw, SSJE
Fifteenth Bishop of Massachusetts
Episcopal Visitor,
Order of Saint Anne—Bethany

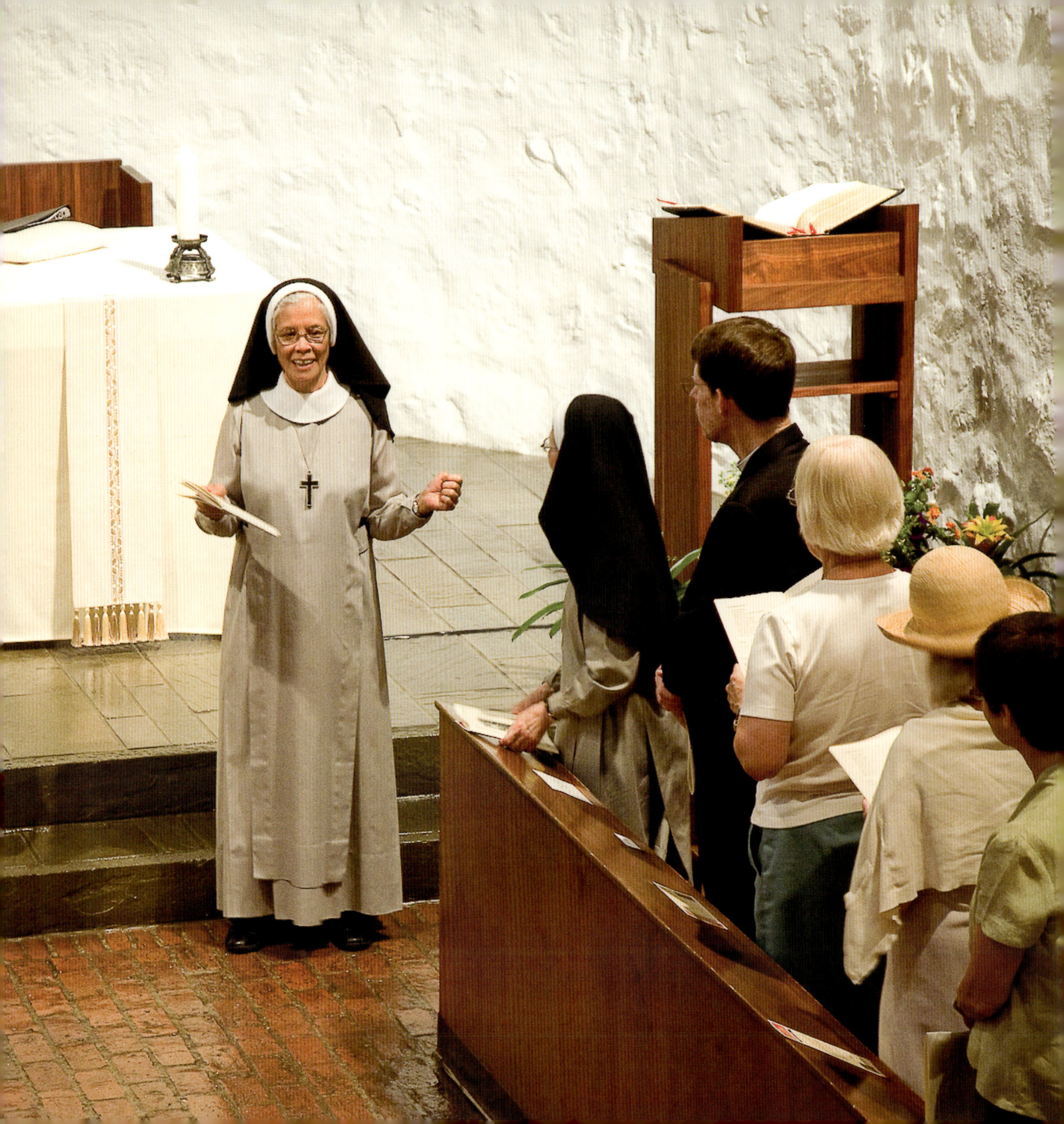

Welcome

Welcome to our celebration! The Sisters of Saint Anne are so thankful to be able to celebrate a hundred years of our Order. One way we can do that is to share with you some of our story. It begins here in Arlington, with Mother Etheldred and Father Powell, and reaches all over the world. There is much more to tell. A hundred years is a long time, and our Sisters have prayed and worked in many places. This small book cannot possibly say everything, but we hope it shows a little of our heritage.

Yes, we have lived and ministered all over the world. We five remaining Sisters at Bethany, along with the Sisters of the Chicago community, continue to feel part of our past, and proud of our past, and very hopeful for our future. Every day we are encouraged and strengthened for God's continued desires for us, with the love and assistance all around us—from our Bishops, the Brothers of the Society of Saint John the Evangelist, the clergy who serve at our altar, our Alongsiders, the Colleagues of the Bethany House of Prayer, our Associates and relations and friends, the children who are part of our life—from all of them. Our blessings overflow. For their words and deeds we are ever so grateful. They give us even more reason to celebrate.

God bless you all.

Sister Ana Clara, OSA
Superior, The Order of Saint Anne—Bethany

Sister Ana Clara joined the Order of Saint Anne at Upi in 1964. Since 1992 she has been the Superior of the Bethany convent in Arlington. The facing page shows her welcoming the congregation at the Eucharist celebrating St Anne's Day, 2008; above, with her godson Luke Haig Griffin.

Antiphon on Magnificat · II Vespers

ast en O

mothers, make

haste O

daugh-ters,

Mother Etheldred and 'The Small House at Arlington'

Every Sister of Saint Anne has promised to be, so far as in her lies, a mother to God's children, caring for them as Anne cared for Mary and training them, as she trained her daughter, to fulfill in their lives the will of God. Thousands of children have known how faithfully the Order of Saint Anne has kept that promise for the last hundred years.

Children, it could be said, got the order started—children from the neighborhood in Arlington Heights where Miss Etheldred Breeze Barry lived. She was an author and an illustrator of children's books, who modeled her drawings on neighborhood children. The girls and boys who came to the studio in her house to pose for her became, in time, a kind of club. It was not the ordinary kind of club, though. Other clubs have clubrooms: this one had a chapel. Miss Barry fitted out an upstairs room in her house with benches, Prayer Books, and a tiny altar complete with candles and a crucifix. She was herself a devout Episcopalian, who put her 'high church' convictions into practice as an Associate of the Society of Saint Margaret and a Sunday School teacher at the Church of the Advent in Boston. The children in Arlington, as she later wrote, would 'learn more from the Church Service than from anything I could teach them,' but she gave them instruction too, drawn from the 'Penny Catechism.' Although this was a Roman Catholic booklet, Miss Barry was convinced that the same religion it taught could be found, with some searching perhaps, in the Book of Common Prayer. Some parents, she knew, might object—as indeed they did—but she was loath to make a secret of her work and sent copies of the catechism home with the older children. As a result she was sometimes able to teach their parents too. In the chapel there were caps for the girls to wear, saints days were observed, and at Christmas a crèche appeared. Before long there was not enough space, and Miss Barry's thoughts turned to putting up a separate building. Such a project was beyond her means, but hopeful plans were drawn up, and the children began to collect pennies. They also added to their prayers a collect she composed. Three

Things of Good Report

The children who came to pose for me in my studio had been gathered into a small club. I had been distressed by the stories they told me, of crimes and scandals, which their mothers read to them from the daily papers, and I suggested that instead they look for reports of deeds of kindness and courage, which I would much prefer to hear…It was a very enthusiastic club, and it was surprising the number of cuttings they found. I lettered the verse… from Philippians IV 8, and tacked it up on the studio door, and the children said it in unison at the end of each club meeting.

Whatsoever things are true, whatsoever things are honest, whatsoever things are just, whatsoever things are pure, whatsoever things are lovely, whatsoever things are of good report…think on these things.

Mother Etheldred, OSA
autograph account of the Order's early years

Sundays after they had begun saying it, the father of two of the boys paid a call on her to volunteer his labor. To lower the expense, he arranged for lumber to be brought directly from Maine and helped to saw it. The following Spring saw a procession making its way from Miss Barry's house to the Chapel of the Holy Child that stood, newly built, in her garden. Behind boys vested in cassock and cotta, one of whom had a censer to swing, came a priest from the Society of Saint John the Evangelist in Boston carrying the vessels for Mass. 'It was the first time, I think,' Miss Barry writes, 'that Mass had been celebrated in Arlington Heights … I thought God had blessed me to the fullest extent, and could have nothing more in store. How little I knew!'

What she did not know was that soon, together with the priest who first presided in the little wooden chapel, she would establish the Order of Saint Anne.

The priest was the Revd Frederick Cecil Powell, SSJE who has a section of his own in this book. The Order of Saint Anne honors him as its Father Founder, and Mother Etheldred, as Miss Barry became, always referred to him so. But she also records that it was he who asked her, 'Has it occurred to you that God may be calling *you* to found a new Community?' At the time, she was discerning her own vocation, and hesitating between two paths, or what she thought were two. One of them was the religious life of a nun; the other, her own 'little flock' of children in Arlington. The idea that the two callings might be combined came from Fr Powell. He had already taken responsibility for several abandoned or neglected children in Boston, finding homes and caregivers for them wherever he could. The need for such a ministry was great, and Fr Powell began to envision a permanent home for it. In 1909 Miss Barry offered to donate her house for the purpose. According to one account, Fr Powell looked at her thoughtfully and said, 'I will accept it on one condition.' And what, she asked, was that? 'The condition is that you give yourself with the house.'

So it was that 'the small house at Arlington'—named in allusion to the title of one of Trollope's famous 'Barchester' novels—became St John's House. What had been Miss Barry's studio became a dormitory. After six months, the new enterprise announced itself to the world, in the shape of the first issue of GEMS, a little monthly magazine that took its name from the initials of Gertrude, Eva, and Maude, the first three children. As might be expected, the announcement included an appeal for donations, along with what would now be called a mission statement. 'Our aim is to make a home in which children whose parents are either dead or obliged to leave them in order to work, may be loved and cared for.' From then on, to love and care for children would be the mission of the Order of Saint Anne.

More children had arrived, and soon another house on the same block, renamed St Mary's, was purchased.

THE FIRST BABY ARRIVES

January 19. Today Christopher MacFadden came to us—a month old today—and today he was christened, with all the children and Sisters around him. We thought of S. Christopher carrying the Christ Child that stormy Christmas Eve. We thought also of Christ Himself, the Great Shepherd, taking this little lamb in his arms.

'Memorabilia' in GEMS, 1911

St John's House, the 'small house at Arlington,' from a 1910 issue of GEMS.

Miss Barry herself, however, characteristically observes that what to her was a far more important event was the reservation of the Blessed Sacrament in the chapel. The Order had not yet been founded in a formal sense, but the intention was there from the first. Miss Barry was already committed to a rule of life, composed by Fr Albert Edward Tovey, SSJE, her spiritual director. She and the women who helped with the 'waifs and strays' rose at five, recited the liturgical Office of Prime together, woke the children, and after breakfast said Morning Prayer and sent them off to school. At one point it seemed that financial difficulties would make it impossible to continue the work with children unless the idea of a religious community was abandoned. Rather than turn away those who had already given up a great deal to join her, Miss Barry took up illustrating once again, although she no longer had a studio. Finding time to draw was difficult too, and she had to take her work with her on retreat.

At last, on 22 November 1910, she and two others, the original members of the Order, were clothed as Sister Etheldred, Sister Monica, and Sister Anne. They had been too busy with the children to sew their own religious habits, but the design was Sister Etheldred's. She also designed the cross they wore, made of black wood surrounded with silver—'the cross with a halo.' In this case Fr Powell 'kindly gave way,' though he would have preferred an iron cross. He did not always give way. Relations between the two founders seem to have been cordial, and always deferential on Sister Etheldred's part, but sometimes strained and occasionally painful. The root of the tension was perhaps in part a difference as to which of two ideals of the religious life should take precedence—active or contemplative, Leah or Rachel, works of mercy or the practice of prayer. Sister Etheldred had always longed for the life of an 'enclosed' nun. She was perfectly capable of helping to nail shingles on the roof of the new chapel, and she was to prove herself resourceful, more than once, in finding means of support for the Order. Yet at the same time her reports on visits to other communities dwell on how the Offices were sung, and her devotion to Christ present in the Sacrament appears in her writing again and again. Fr Powell would not, of course, have disagreed in principle with any of this. His, though, was a more pragmatic temperament. He took very seriously the maxim that *laborare est orare,* to work is to pray, and there was more than enough work that needed doing.

About a year after the first Sisters 'took the veil,' Fr Powell proposed to add a third leg to what, in his words, had been a two-legged stool. The two were the Sisters themselves and the Associates of the Order, whom the Sisters had called on for financial support to the point of wearying them. To these would be added Sisters who would live under vows but would not wear the habit. Their secular employment would earn money for the Order. Fr Powell thought this an excellent innovation, which other communities would want to imitate. All but one of the Sisters thought otherwise, however, and so did some of the Cowley Fathers. The ensuing months were 'a very sad time,' as Sister Etheldred's account puts it. Fr Powell was far from pleased with the resistance his plan was encountering, while the Sisters, for their part, lost confidence in him, at least for the moment. At this point in her narrative Sister Etheldred states simply: 'Father Powell removed me from my office of Sister-in-Charge, and put the junior Novice in my place.' She offers no further comment, except praise for Sister Ursula, who replaced her: 'how hard she tried to make peace and goodwill, not only among the Sisters in Arlington, but between the two Houses.'

The 'two Houses' were St John's House in Arlington and a house on Temple Street in Boston, behind the Cowley Fathers' mission church, which had been 'opened in the name of the Sisters of St. Anne' and would be called St Anne's House. Fr Powell had gone

The oratory chapel on the second floor of Etheldred Barry's home, which became St John's House.

ahead with his idea, although one important change was made. Instead of a single community with some Sisters who worked at secular jobs, there was a First and a Second Order. Both divisions had the same Rule, and postulants for the Second Order were admitted at the chapel in Arlington. But it was soon settled that St Anne's House was not to be a 'cell' of St John's House: it would be an independent foundation.

Etheldred Barry was not only an illustrator but an author in her own right. The cover of her children's book *Little Tong's Mission*.

The timber chapel under construction in Etheldred Breeze Barry's garden. The man on the right is thought to be Lieutenant Richardson, who arranged to have the lumber delivered to Arlington from Maine, and sawed it for building together with a Mr. Doe, left. Mrs Richardson and Miss Barry helped to shingle the roof.

One of Etheldred Barry's illustrations for *The Giant Scissors* by Annie Fellow Johnston, first published in Boston in 1898.

The Chapel of the Holy Child. Children from Miss Barry's club and Sunday school gathered stones that were used in the piers.

Mother Etheldred and 'The Small House at Arlington' 19

An illustration by Mother Etheldred showing a child at the gate to St John's House.

Interlude: A Place with Welcome at Its Heart

I first learned of the Order of Saint Anne in the summer of 1955 when I was in graduate school at Harvard. To eke out my meager resources, I had been blessed with a job as a teaching assistant and 'housemother' in a women's dorm. I was a new Episcopalian and had no idea that religious orders existed in my new church. To my surprise one morning I encountered an old friend from undergraduate days at the University of Kansas—in a gray habit! I knew her as Beverly Dodds, but now she was Sister Christopher. She was taking a summer course and had a ride into Cambridge that made her arrive much too early, so she sat and waited patiently until class time. The Sisters were delighted when Beverly (I was still getting used to calling her by her strange new name) and I decided that she could come and sit in my room while she waited—apparently it just wasn't seemly for a novice to be sitting for extended periods on a bench in Harvard Yard.

We truly enjoyed being reacquainted. Two girls from Kansas! Neither of us could imagine that our lives would take this course and that we would find each other in the beehive that was Harvard Summer School. Soon she invited me to Benediction and supper at the convent. Sister Benedicta was guest mistress then and welcomed me as if I were one of the family. But I had never been in a religious house before so I experienced mild panic that I would walk through the wrong door or sit when I should kneel or do something clumsy that marked me as a tourist in this holy place. And genuflecting was a whole new concept.

But soon the Sunday afternoon visits became frequent, indeed always a bit like coming home. I'd board the trolley in Harvard Square, rattle my way to Arlington, and climb up the hill to the convent. I suspect that Sister Christopher enjoyed my visits because Sister Benedicta usually gave us fresh cookies. A treat! Between meals! Then Beverly/Christopher and I would sit in the garden on pleasant days or find a cozy corner in the convent—and just talk. We were both at a threshold place in our lives so we never ran out of material.

I married, completed my degree, and moved to Washington. The years in Cambridge became a memory of a really golden time. Sister Christopher, then Mother Christopher and I lost touch with each other. Years later I offered a workshop in the Boston area, and my hosts housed me at the convent. The Sisters who had welcomed me so lovingly fifty years before had crossed the great Second Threshold. But I was received—again, and typically—like one of the children come home. Then in March 2007 I offered a weekend retreat at Bethany House. For me it was a time of joy as I realized that the great span of years didn't matter and that I had never really left this place with love and welcome at its heart.

The Revd Margaret Guenther

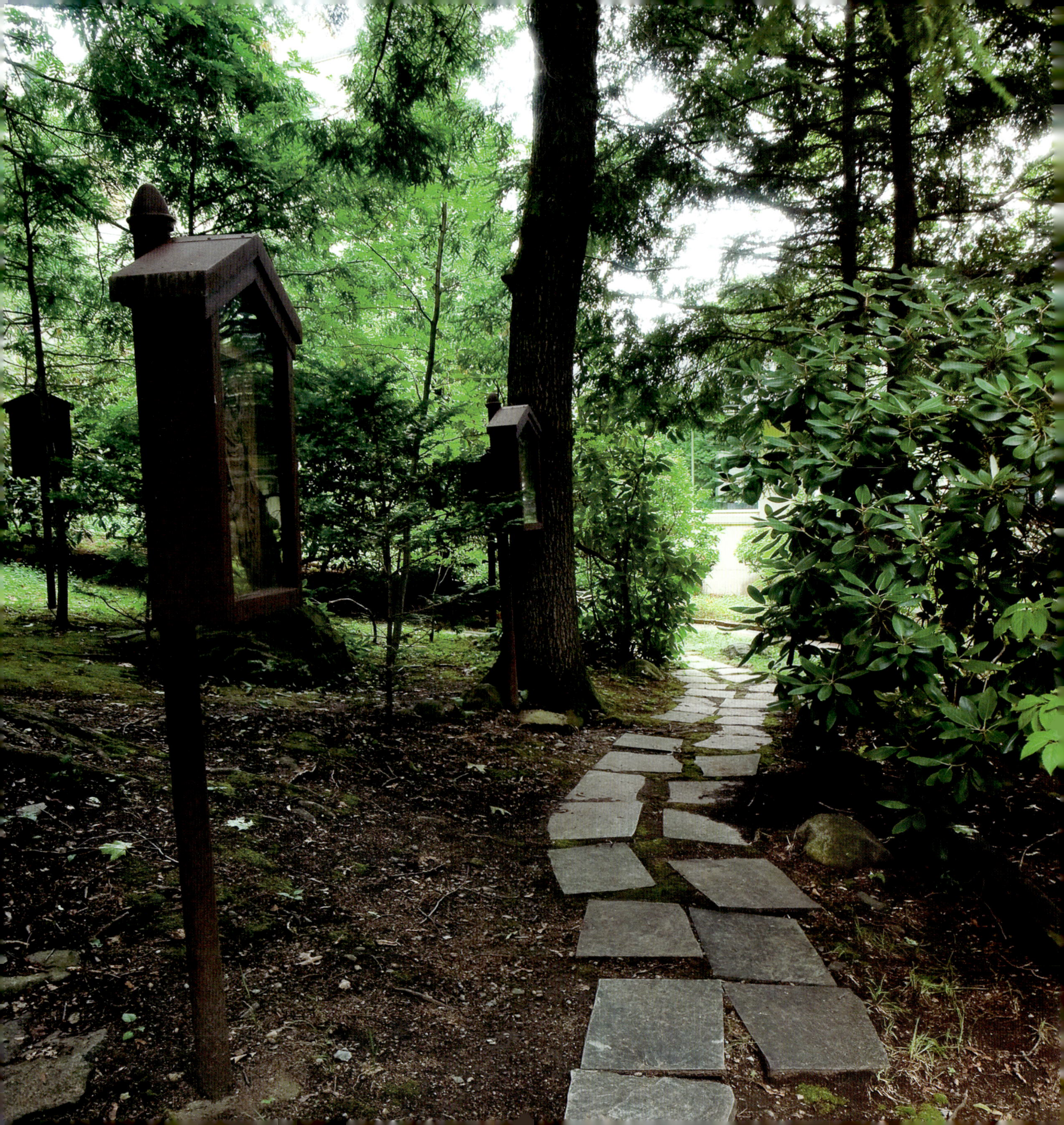

2 The St Anne's School

It was never easy to describe what grew up on the hillside in Arlington Heights, or exactly what was going on there. There were Sisters of Saint Anne. There were children. Together they made up—what? An orphanage? St John's House might have been so described, especially at first. A village? Yes, before long. In 1911, besides the 'small house at Arlington,' two others had been added on Claremont Avenue, St Mary's and St Joseph's, and in 1914 St Raphael's was built as an infirmary. Eventually, the Sisters found themselves operating what was at once a day camp, a nursery, a school, and—most of all—a home. A sketch-map of the grounds drawn in 1923 shows a gymnasium, an orchard, a hen-run, a swimming pool, a clothes yard, a kitchen garden, and a playground with swings and a tennis court. Near the west end of the new stone chapel stands the first of the fourteen outdoor Stations of the Cross, arranged in a winding route that makes its way around the sacristy, eastward across the grounds to Hillside Avenue, and back to the other end of the chapel.

In the early years, children in the Sisters' care left for school in the morning and came home at the end of the day. Then in 1928 St Anne's School was established. At first it offered classes for the youngest children, then expanded to include students through the sixth grade, and in time was educating girls of high-school age. Some of the boarders enrolled in the Lower School lived in the 'Baby Dorm,' which kept the name it had been given in the days when the Sisters took in orphaned infants. Senior students lived in St Mary's House. Each of the dormitories had one of the Sisters living there as house mother. Sister Germaine, for example, who as the business teacher taught typing and shorthand, also served as house mother to sixth- and seventh-grade students, until she became Mother Superior of the convent. Other Sisters were assigned to the study hall and other activities requiring supervision. It was reported that students could tell which of the Sisters was walking the halls, by the way her rosary beads clicked in time with her footsteps. There were nicknames, of course, some of them more affectionate than others. Sister Scholastica was known as 'Sister Elastic,' Sister Maria Dolorosa as 'Sister Double Roses,' and Sister Anne Mary as 'Sam,' from her initials. For Sunday Mass and Benediction in the Chapel, the girls wore capes, sewn by one of the Sisters—red for 'Baby Dorm' students, and later on blue for the Upper School.

In the 1960s local school districts as well as the state's Department of Social Services were beginning to rely on St Anne's School to provide an alternative environment for young women who could not benefit from the public school system, owing to family difficulties or behavioral problems. The School was changing, and as the student handbook for 1973 observed, 'the Order of Saint Anne is likewise living and growing, ready to learn and profit from the past, yet simultaneously preparing to forge into the future, allowing the works of the

Sisters to be molded by the times and thus fulfill the mission of the community to love God by loving mankind, and to manifest this love in the way that best meets the circumstances of an ever changing world.'

By the late 1970s, the Commonwealth of Massachusetts was paying all the students' tuition fees. But it was also becoming clear that the traditional boarding school pattern could not provide all the support these young people needed, and the Sisters were not equipped to develop the more structured programs that were called for. After much thought and many prayers, their decision was to let the School become a distinct institution in its own right, legally separate from the Order of Saint Anne. In 1979 the newly constituted Board of Directors called Mr David Hirshberg as Executive Director, and the following year the School began the next phase of its work, as a residential treatment center.

The name chosen to mark this new beginning also commemorates the past. 'The Germaine Lawrence School' honors both Mother Germaine, who was devoted to the work of the School throughout her many years in the convent, and the many members of her family, the Lawrences, who supported that work in numberless ways.

A Sister walking with students near the Chinese bell.

Goblin Confessions

Religion is the very atmosphere of the Convent, and its practice as natural as breathing. Nothing surprises us, therefore: but it is a little startling to hear the Sister Principal announce at Assembly: 'Play practice will be as usual today; goblins will dance at three o'clock, and so must make their confessions first.'

Gems, *Fall 1947*

24   Catch the Vision

Interlude: Lives Knit Together

The Sisters of Saint Anne saved my life, and then enriched it beyond measure.

I first met them as a rebellious young teen in 1961, when I was banished to boarding school. Within weeks, I was captured by the Sisters' warmth and joy, their sense of order, their encouragement, and their life of simple beauty. After my first year, my family wanted me to return home. I refused. I was blessed.

With the Sisters I broke bread as a student, a Novice, an Associate, a parishioner, an employee (as the school morphed into a treatment center in the 1970s), and a long-time friend. I remember Sister Evelyn marching for civil rights, Sister Helena and Sister Augusta as they journeyed to and from China, the festive arrivals and sad departures of the Philippines Sisters, the beginning and end of Bethany in Lincoln, the church's ecumenical burst in the 1960s, and the chapel renovations.

Who could forget Sister Ruth, our commanding Headmistress? Or Sister Theodora's beautiful Angel Garden, and her ability to silence with a glance a hundred girls in study hall? Or Sister Marie Therese's strong wisdom and her ability to see the good in everyone and everything? Or Mother Miriam's calm, warm leadership, Jeanne Sproat's energy and intellect, the devotion of each of the Sisters and the lay staff who poured themselves into the school?

Our daily lives were knit together with traditions—May Day, the Christmas pageant, chapel each day and twice on Sunday, capes and beanies, the Angelus, 'Seldom Seen,' 'Heights Privileges,' and dances, plays, teas. Today, tradition continues. The energy of sixty Sisters is now embodied in five faithful members of the Order who by their very existence carry the love of Christ and the gifts of Saint Anne's forward. I am overjoyed to be part of their celebration of praise and thanksgiving for all of the lives transformed by their ministry and all whom we have touched because of them!

Cheryl Cronin
Class of 1964, St Anne's School

Sister Marie Therese reading with a student at St. Anne's School.

CHRIST WITH CHILDREN

3 Children

The order of Saint Anne's *Rule of Life* suggests
that there should be children in every house of the Order.
'They educate the Sisters as much as the Sisters educate them.'

A child at the 'wishing well' on the grounds of the convent.

HOPE RICHMOND

A Baby, of all people, has appeared at the Convent in response to the invitation, in our last issue, to a fairy. Her name is Hope Richmond. We drew her attention to the fact of it being expressly stated that we did not need any more babies. She said that she was only one baby, and but three weeks old at that, and if we had room for a fairy, we surely had room for her.

GEMS, *June 1919*

The man who marries Hope Richmond may not know it until too late, but he will find that he has wedded not so much a morning star as a morning alarm clock. From that time forth he'll have no more chance against rising in the world than a stone with a near-by derrick.

GEMS, *October 1926*

OPPOSITE: 'Christ with Children,' marble sculpture by Louis Lualdi in what was formerly the porch of St. Anne's Chapel. Carved in 1957, it originally stood at an outside altar.

Gunesh Gery (*née* Guran) as a child, dressed for a play at the School.

Ethel and Selina in the rose-garden

The Rt Revd Bud Cederholm, Bishop Suffragan of Massachusetts, blessing the children's garden on Clergy Family Day at Bethany, 2009.

Somethings to Do

Allene Smith, dainty as a porcelain flower from the garden of a mandarin, sweeter than the rose-encumbered June, is digging worms for the birds. Who would not be in a happy state of Pooh, who, one day finding that he had nothing to do thought he 'would do something.' There are so many nice somethings to do. The very sight of young Smith brings that astonishment which is awakened by the yearly upthrust of the crocus spears, flashing with laughter and innocent mirth against the cold curtain of winter. The child's speech is swift and light like her footsteps.

Gems, *August 1929*

Wet Paint

Our babies are the greatest charm and wonder here, but the children—the older boys and girls—they also are worth watching. They are so happy! There beyond the trees are Harold and Wilfrid. They have just discovered a newly painted gate in front of S.Mary's House. They stop and gaze, and consult together. How can they best make use of such a find? Will any one notice if they put out their fingers, just to see how wet the paint is? And how would it look on Dorothy's nose?

Gems, *1911*

Hope Tremblay (*née* Richmond) during her schooldays.

Sunday morning

Neighborhood children at the Mission of St Francis of Assisi at Upi, Philippines.

Children 29

Interlude: Where Your Treasure Is

When I was ten years old, I was introduced to St Anne's School through my uncle, the Rt Revd Kenneth A. Viall, SSJE, who had been one of the Cowley Fathers' missionaries in Japan. He had brought back two kimonos as presents for my brother and sister, and later asked if the Sisters at the school could borrow them for the annual Christmas play. My mother agreed, of course, and suggested that the family should attend the performance, to see the kimonos being worn. That was the beginning of my parents' plans for me to be a student there.

My six years at St Anne's School began in 1946, on the Saturday before all the other girls arrived. There was just one other student to talk to. The first Sister I encountered was the house mother of the 'top floor dormitory,' Sister Germaine. The next day was Sunday, so there was a service in the chapel—Mass, which began at seven o'clock, *before* breakfast. Sister Germaine made sure I knew it was not enough simply to curtsey on entering and leaving the chapel: I *must* genuflect. Having come from a 'low church' Episcopalian background, all this was something of a culture-shock. But most of the new students had to learn new 'high church' behavior, and we all survived the trauma.

Mother Germaine, OSA.

I had grown up in a neighborhood where many children went to Roman Catholic parochial schools, and the stories they told about nuns were rather nightmarish, especially where punishment (usually administered with a ruler) was concerned. At St Anne's School there was strict discipline, but no corporal punishment. A misbehaving student would 'lose marks' according to the severity of her offence, and losing too many meant losing certain privileges. In very serious cases, the Sister in charge might have to send a student to the Reverend Mother. Despite her fearsome title, Mother Miriam presented herself as a jolly, down-to-earth person. Students sometimes reported that they liked being sent to her, because she would talk to them kindly and gave them lollipops. (So much for corporal punishment!)

One Sister that many of us did hold in awe was the principal, Sister Ruth. She was English, bred up under the English system of education, very strict, and very serious about her duties as Sister Principal. Yet she too had her soft spot, when the opportunity came to talk with her one-to-one. The Christmas play and the spring play were Sister Ruth's ideas, and she sewed the costumes for both. The spring play was really an interpretive dance production, performed in the main garden of the convent, and required the participation of every student.

Among our favorite teachers was Sister Julian, who once confided in me that she was only one step ahead of her students in chemistry and biology—but I can attest from my college experience that she prepared us superbly in both those sciences. Sister was a very talented singer as well. It was reported that when she left Colorado, she had meant to travel to New York and audition for the Metropolitan Opera, but continued her journey and ended it at Saint Anne's Convent. At that time there was no organ in the chapel and all the singing was *a capella,* led by Sister's beautiful, soaring, operatic soprano voice.

What did I gain from St Anne's School? Perhaps its biggest effect was a deep sense of spirituality in my life. I developed a sense of the profound meaning of prayer. In 1955, when I was in my senior year of college, there was an epidemic of polio and I was one of those it struck. The Sisters prayed for me daily. I think every one of them wrote to me in hospital. Dear Sister Julian wrote every single day. I continue to consider the Sisters among my best friends, and cannot imagine my life without them, even today. 'Where your treasure is, there will your heart be also.'

Prof. Jacqueline G. Haslett
Class of 1952, St Anne's School

Two pages from a book of antiphons, written out, illuminated, and bound by Mother Etheldred. The plainsong she so loved had medieval origins, and she delighted in emulating the calligraphy and decoration that medieval scribes used in liturgical volumes.

4 The Religious Life in Anglicanism

As a community of women living under vows, the Order of Saint Anne belongs to a tradition nearly as old as Christianity. As a religious order within the Anglican Communion, it belongs to a more recent tradition as well. Although there are now a number of such orders, they are all comparatively new. The Church of England, from which the Episcopal Church and the other Anglican churches derive in different ways, had rid itself of convents and monasteries in the sixteenth century, distancing itself from the Bishop of Rome by doing so. Not until the early 1800s was there such a thing as an Anglican nun, and when Sisters did reappear Anglicans were not always ready to welcome them back.

The revival of the religious life was an important aspect of what is known as the Catholic Movement in Anglicanism. The word 'Catholic' has never meant only 'Roman Catholic.' Anglicans have always maintained that theirs is as much a Catholic as it is a Protestant form of Christianity. Or at least that is what they have maintained in principle. Supporters of the Catholic Movement, however, felt that in practice the principle had been lost sight of, and they set out to reclaim for Anglicanism a religious heritage which, in their view, had been neglected for too long.

Little by little, followers of the Movement began to introduce—or restore, as they preferred to say—teachings and practices that Anglicanism had for the most part abandoned. They advocated private confession, on the authority of a disused rubric in the Book of Common Prayer. They emphasized the importance of the sacraments, especially Holy Communion, which they soon began to speak of by its traditional name, the Mass. They stressed that members of the clergy should be referred to as priests and addressed as 'Father.' Their teachings found visible expression in rituals and ceremonies that were strikingly different from what Anglicans were used to—celebrating the Eucharist weekly or even daily, wearing the traditional Mass vestments instead of cassock and surplice, fasting before Communion, burning candles and incense, keeping saints' days, making the sign of the cross, and reserving the Blessed Sacrament, both for private devotion and for the extraliturgical service of Benediction.

Today, few of these practices would be regarded as eccentric. A Eucharist every Sunday is now the norm among Episcopalians, and weekday celebrations are common. Choirs wear vestments, priests wear chasubles, and bishops wear miters. All this goes to show how successful the Catholic Movement was in the long run. When it began, however, it met with suspicion and hostility. Anglicans had been accustomed to define their church by what it was not, and what it was emphatically not was Roman Catholic. Hard though it is to imagine, riots started because a cross—a plain cross—had been set on an Anglican altar, and more than one Anglican priest was jailed for ceremonial offences like swinging a censer in church. Faced with forceful and widespread opposition, those who agreed with the Catholic Movement closed ranks and became a party, which like every party was fiercely loyal to what its members considered essential—in this case, to what were judged to be the essential teachings and practices of a properly Catholic church. There had always been more or less 'high church' Anglicans. Now there were Anglo-Catholics.

Although 'advanced' ceremonial was a flashpoint, it was certainly not the only thing the Catholic Movement stood for. 'You cannot claim to worship Jesus in the Tabernacle if you do not pity Jesus in the slum.' So said a prominent Anglo-Catholic bishop, Frank Weston of Zanzibar. The pageantry and piety of Anglo-Catholic worship was closely bound up with ministry to 'the least of these,' Christ's brothers and sisters. That is why religious orders were revived. As early as 1839, Edward Bouverie Pusey, one of the pioneers of the Catholic Movement, urged that the Church of England needed organized 'sisters of charity' like the Sœurs de Charité founded by St Vincent de Paul. Appropriately, it was Pusey who received the vows of Marian Rebecca Hughes, who may be said to have reinstated the religious life within the Anglican church. At the time, she had neither a community nor a superior, but she went on to found the Convent of the Holy and Undivided Trinity in Oxford. Other orders for women followed—a new one every other year, on average, through the end of the nineteenth century. It was jokingly said that founding a sisterhood was a *sine qua non* for any Anglo-Catholic priest worth his salt.

In the terminology of the religious life, the early Anglican sisterhoods were either 'active' or 'mixed,' as the Order of Saint Anne would be, rather than exclusively 'contemplative.' Their members lived together in community and together recited the traditional Offices of corporate prayer, but they combined this daily round of liturgical worship with service to the poor and needy, especially in urban slums. They ran soup kitchens, set up hostels, founded 'ragged schools' and orphanages. At a time when nursing was neither a science nor a profession, they visited and cared for the sick. The order known as the Devonport Sisters became famous for their work during outbreaks of cholera. Theirs was also the first order to adopt the practice of daily Communion, which had had not been seen in the Church of England since the sixteenth century.

At first the religious orders met with some of the same hostility as did other aspects of the Catholic Movement. Despite their good works, sisterhoods were denounced from the pulpit and in the public press as 'Jesuit,' a code-word in those days for all that was perceived to be despicable, superstitious, and crafty in the Roman Catholic Church. Particularly offensive was the idea that women should even be allowed, let alone encouraged, to take any lifelong vow other than the vows of marriage. Nor were attitudes any different in

The Religious Life

'The Religious Life cannot put anything into one that is not there already. It is like the varnish on wood,' and he laid his hand on the back of the pew where he was sitting. 'It brings out and shows all that is there—the lights and the darks.'

F.C. Powell, SSJE, as reported by Mother Etheldred, OSA

The involvement in social activism that was a hallmark of the 'Catholic Movement' in Anglicanism has continued. In the spring of 1965, Sisters from the Order of Saint Anne took part in the third Selma-to-Montgomery Civil Rights March. Before they left for Alabama, the Boston *Record American* published a photograph (*top*) of Sister Germaine with Elliot Richardson, then the Lieutenant Governor of Massachusetts, checking the news of a tribute to the Revd James Reeb, a Boston minister killed on the second march.

The Religious Life in Anglicanism 35

HOMELINESS

There are more ornate residences than S. John's House, Arlington Heights, more resplendent homes than S. Anne's House, 44 Temple Street, Boston, more magnificent country houses than S. Augustine's Farm, Foxboro, but nowhere in the world, and never in time, have there stood abodes more fitting for their purpose. They are a witness to the basic simplicity, clean beauty, homeliness, friendliness, and neighbourliness of the Religious Life as lived without bolts or bars, high walls or hedges, in poor homes among poor people in town, suburb, and country.

F.C. Powell, SSJE, in 'A Guide Book, or Microcosmographia Religiosa,' 1923

America. That is probably why a guide book published by the Order of Saint Anne makes a point of observing that 'the extension of responsibility through time' by making promises 'is what chiefly distinguishes us from brutes and reptiles. … The vow is to the Christian what the song is to the bird or the bark to the dog; his voice, whereby he is known.'

Much has changed since the heyday of Anglo-Catholicism in the 1920s. Neither the church nor the culture which it exists to transform has stood still. The Anglican sisterhoods began as part of a Movement which, at its outset and for a long time afterwards, was deliberately hierarchical, paternalistic, authoritarian, and clerical. Like the clergy, members of the women's orders adopted a distinctive dress and a distinctive title, but they were laypeople none the less, and female as well. Every right-minded Anglo-Catholic, themselves included, would have thought of them as being under the authority of ordained men. That way of seeing

A watercolor drawing by Mother Etheldred, intended for reproduction as a holy card. It shows children visiting the outdoor shrine of Our Lady at the convent. The statue, a replica of one in the crypt at Chartres Cathedral, was given in 1911.

36 ଛ Catch the Vision

The original artwork for another of Mother Etheldred's many holy cards. Girls from St. Anne's School, in their red capes and hoods, are gathered for a blessing of the garden at Rogationtide.

things eroded, slowly at first, as the twentieth century went on. The opportunities for Christian ministry that are now open to women in most parts of the Anglican church would have been unimaginable a hundred years ago. It seems likely that, if religious orders now have a less significant role in Anglicanism than they once had, and if the number of women's communities is smaller than it was, part of the reason is that their contribution is being made in other ways. At the same time, a broader question has no clear answer yet: how best to uphold, in the twenty-first century, what was most valuable in the Catholic Movement of the nineteenth.

The religious life has been lived within Christianity for almost as long as there have been Christians, but the shape of that life has never been static. Today, as in the past, new forms of intentional community are being tried out. Whatever the future may hold, these words from GEMS are as apt as they were when they were written in 1923:

We must not judge by numbers, or by the perpetuity of association. Neither of these is any criterion. Life, whether natural or spiritual, does not depend upon numbers or length. It is an individual possession. Plants are none the less alive, because, through whatever cause, … [they] leave no successors to perpetuate the species. So a Religious Community may be none the less alive because it existed only for a few years and then passed away.

The Religious Life in Anglicanism ☙ 37

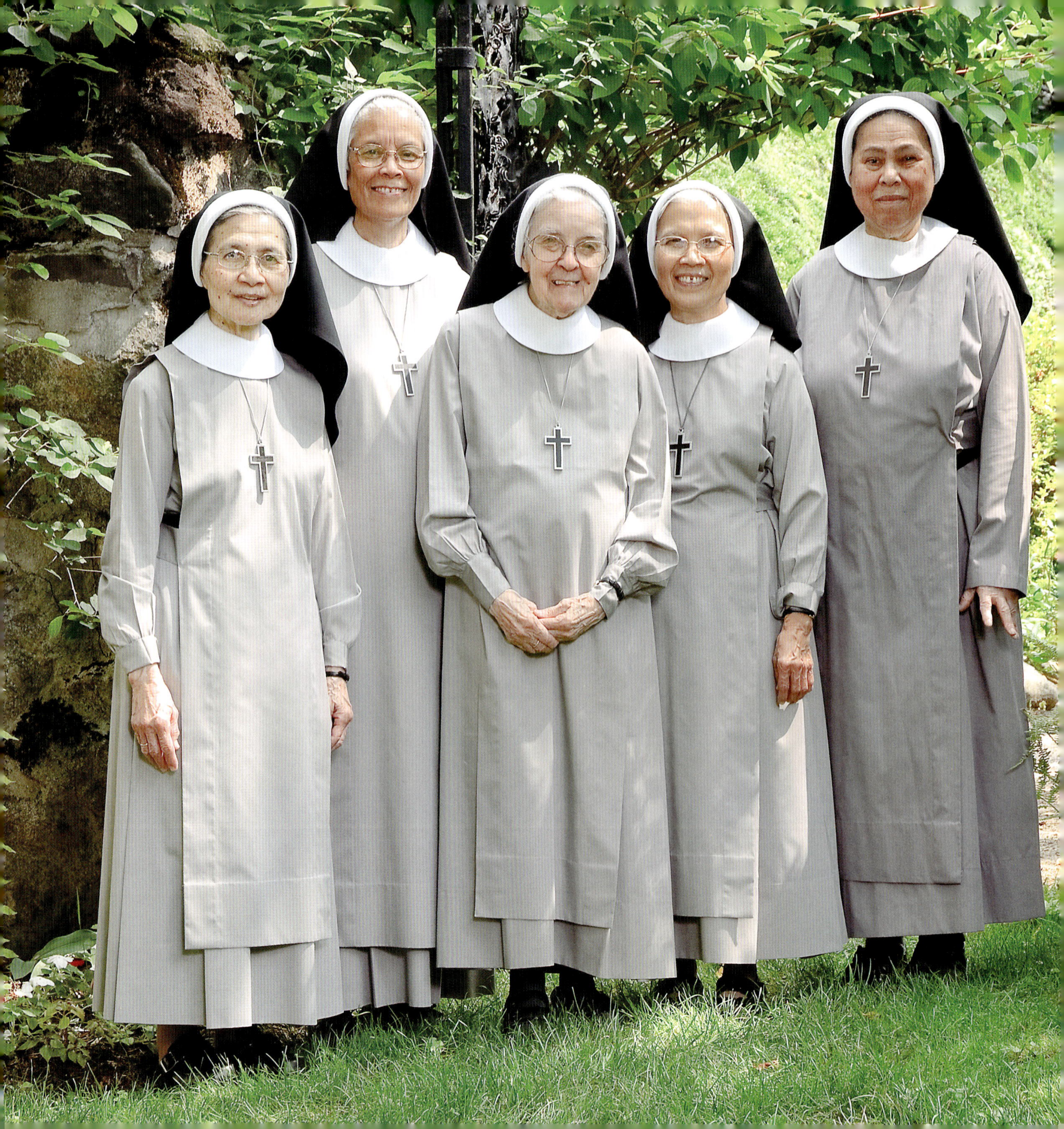

5 Habits

Like so much in the Order of Saint Anne, the original habit worn by professed Sisters was designed by Mother Etheldred (right). According to the Order's Rule of Life, this distinctive dress 'is a symbol of our religious vocation. Within the habit, there should be found the power of a love that is all-transforming. The outward limitations of the habit do but intensify-they cannot narrow-the love of those who are close to the Sacred Heart of Jesus. ... A habit is a protection. So is a high wall around a garden, but a high wall is not of the essence of a garden.' A photograph taken at the Philippines convent shows Sisters wearing the Order's habit in its early form. Today it takes the more informal, less cumbersome form (shown on the facing page) that was adopted in 1970, shortly before the Chapter meeting pictured below. The Sisters' cross is now smaller too, but it is still made of black wood surrounded by silver—'the cross with a halo,' as Mother Etheldred called it a hundred years ago.

Interlude: A Chorus of Women's Voices

While reading a history of the Order of Saint Anne written by Sister Johanna for the seventy-fifth anniversary of the order in 1985, *A Theme For Four Voices*, I remember thinking how the book actually includes many more voices than the title suggests. Each of the women mentioned in the book, from the necrology at the beginning to the last page of the text, was loved by God, was called by God, and lived out her vocation in a unique way, as only she could do. For me the legacy of the Order of Saint Anne is an ongoing 'chorus' of women's voices, reaching back to 1910 and continuing to this day.

My first encounters with the Order were during my years in seminary in the early 1980s. One of my sponsoring clergy was the Revd Canon Jeanne Sproat, formerly a member of OSA in Arlington. She had also attended St Anne's school there as a girl. Jeanne Sproat became an icon to many women seminarians at the time, a role strengthened by her visibility as the first woman ordained to the priesthood in the Diocese of Massachusetts. Despite the climate during those early years of women's ordination in the Episcopal Church, my first meetings with the Bethany Sisters were far less politically charged. I met them several times at the monastery of the Society of Saint John the Evangelist in Cambridge, and we shared in some meals and programs together. During those years the Bethany Sisters were mostly seen in relation to their work caring for developmentally disabled women, some of whom lived with the Ssters for most of their lives.

Clearly, the Bethany Sisters loved these women, 'the girls,' as they referred to them, very deeply. It wasn't until several years later that I realized the toll their ministry was taking on the community itself. It was then that the Sisters asked me to work with them on some community issues and decision-making.

Over the course of a year in the late 1980s I came frequently to Bethany in Lincoln for part of a day and met with the community. The stories of individual sisters are theirs to tell; some of them have carried the stories to heaven with them. My own reflection on their stories and their questions focused on many of the developmental issues faced by all women. Many of the Sisters quite courageously fought their families in order to join the community. Some gave up family ties, their homeland, and their cultures. Within the community, generational differences in regard to the definition of women's roles and options for women religious surfaced, as they did in communities throughout the country, and often caused frustration and hurt feelings. Throughout the history of the Episcopal Church, where the work of women in the church has been recognized, more emphasis is put on

The Revd M. Jeanne Sproat, the first woman ordained to the priesthood in the Diocese of Massachusetts. Before her ordination she was a Sister of the Order of Saint Anne, and before that a student in St Anne's School. From 1980-1988 she was Canon Chaplain in the Diocese, and from then until 1995 Canon Pastor of the Cathedral Church of St Paul, Boston.

opportunities for service than on the affirmation of the women and their religious vocations. It took some time and a great deal of courage before individual Sisters, the majority of whom personally felt it was time for them to cease managing a facility for the developmentally disabled, to come together as a community to make the decision and to begin planning for an alternative future.

History has taught us that all major efforts to enlarge women's vocational options in the Episcopal Church, from sisterhoods, to deaconesses, to lay professionals, to women's ordination, were at first sources of great conflict and resistance. Despite the hazards, women enthusiastically followed these vocations as opportunities to live out their callings, eventually earning some level of respect for their tenacity and dedication. Those of us in the twenty-first century Episcopal Church inherit a more compassionate church because of the Order of Saint Anne. Vocations lived with integrity have a powerful impact on the whole people of God. That the Sisters accomplished so much and created so many meaningful roles for themselves with limited resources and support is testament to the depth of their faith and indomitable spirits.

Maya Angelou wrote, 'History, despite its wrenching pain, cannot be unlived, but if faced with courage, need not be lived again.' The chorus of women's voices of the Order of Saint Anne speak not only to their own age, but to those of us who care deeply for the Episcopal Church now and in the future. Our sense of vocation is what makes us whole. In it lies the conviction that our lives and selves belong to God. Let us build together a vision of the church true to whose we are and who God calls each of us to be.

The Revd Sheryl Kujawa-Holbrook

The 'cross with a halo' in the foreground is worn by professed Sisters of Saint Anne today. It replaced the larger version, as designed by Mother Etheldred, seen in the background. Between them is the cross worn by Postulants.

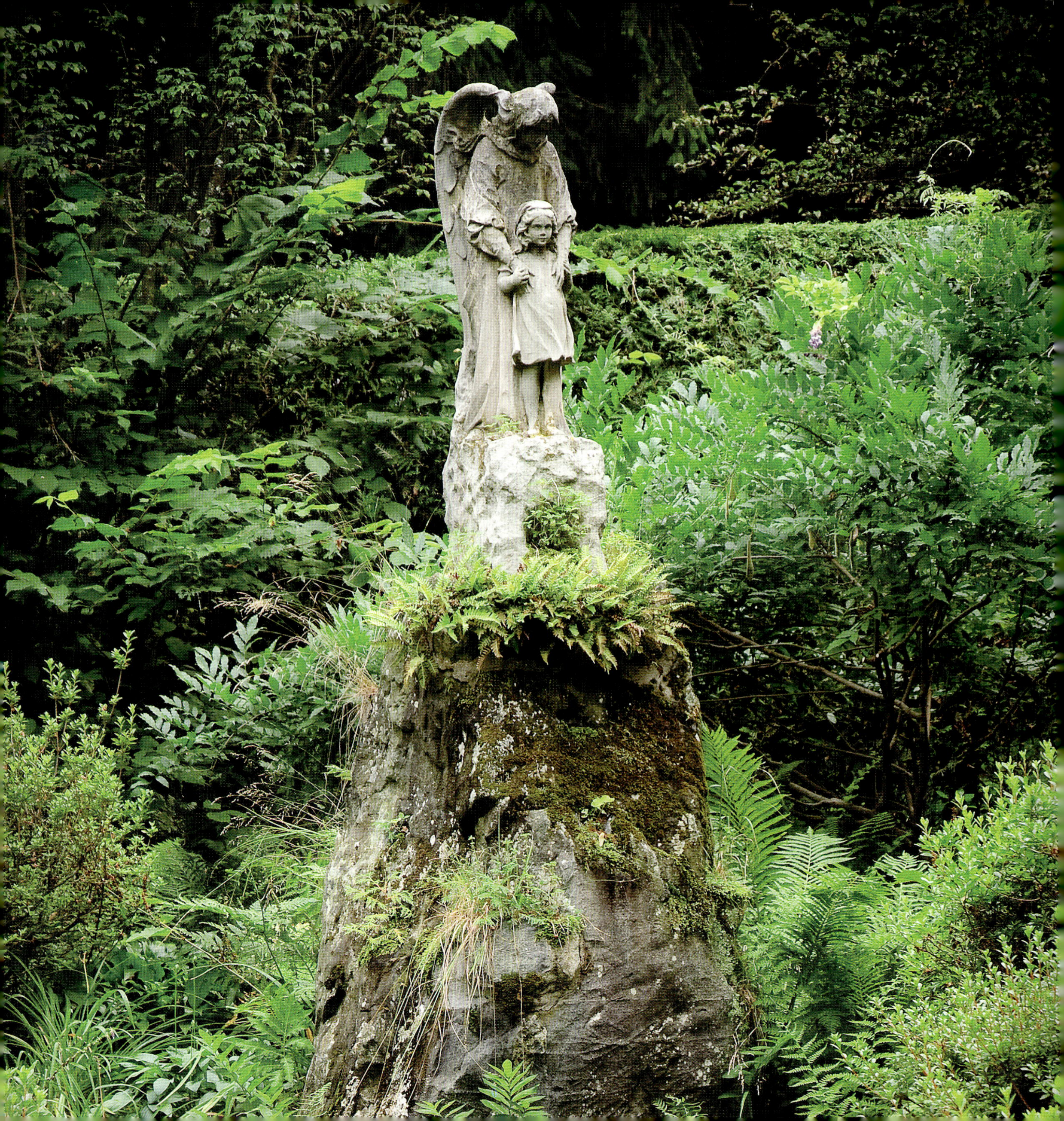

6 The Father Founder

'Some people,' Frederic Cecil Powell wrote, 'collect postage stamps. I collect life.' Among his friends were nobles and nobodies, and his ministry embraced the whole kaleidoscope of humanity, from trapeze artists to Boston Brahmins. But children were his special joy, and homeless children his particular concern. In hospitals where he visited the sick there were unwanted, illegitimate babies. A dying woman implored him to look after her children, whose father had disappeared. Again and again he found homes for these orphans. The families who took them in often belonged to the parish of St John's Church on Bowdoin Street, and one of the parishioners, Louise Rothstein, was put in charge of seeing that the children they cared for were brought up properly. Soon a little leaflet appeared, with prayers for the establishment of a sisterhood devoted to caring for children in need. The answer to those prayers came a few months later, when Etheldred Barry went to Fr Powell and offered to give her house for such work. It was this house that became the Order of Saint Anne's first convent. Miss Barry became the first Mother Superior, Miss Rothstein one of the original Sisters of the Second Order, and Fr Powell the Father Founder.

Powell had been born in England, the son of an Evangelical clergyman, but made his way as a young man to Canada. There, after studying at Trinity College in Toronto, he was ordained. While he was serving as curate in an Ontario parish, he encountered the Society of St John the Evangelist, in the person of its Founder, Richard Meux Benson, and not long afterwards became a 'Cowley Father' himself. Fr Powell was admitted to postulancy at the Society's American house in Boston, and there he returned following his novitiate in Oxford and two years of mission work in South Africa. The Mission House on Bowdoin Street, next door to St John's Church, was to be his home for thirty-seven years.

'All the poor and unlucky, the sick and the helpless, the weak and sinning, every form of human incompetence and misfortune comes ringing our bell,' Powell

A portrait of the Father Founder, Frederick Cecil Powell, SSJE. Formerly at Bethany in Lincoln, it now hangs in the refectory at the Monastery of the Society of Saint John the Evangelist in Cambridge.

OPPOSITE: The Guardian Angel statue, one of many small, separate outdoor spaces planned by Fr Powell on the grounds of the convent. The model for the little girl was Nancy Wilson, one of the children at St John's House, who later married Christopher McFadden, the first baby brought there. The statue stands on a boulder dug up a few yards away.

The Father Founder 43

wrote of the Mission House. He would not have had it otherwise. 'I prefer the squalid, ill-kept thoroughfares, shadowed by tall, smudgy tenement houses, teeming with unprosperous and noisy life (just such a district as we live in).' Yet he loved beauty as well, in nature and art alike, and he saw to it that there was plenty of both at the convent in Arlington. From his travels in England and elsewhere he brought back antique statues and ornaments for the garden, together with pictures and vestments for the chapel. One of his notable friends, Isabella Stuart Gardner, was also a lifelong friend of the Order of Saint Anne, who added works of art from her own collections. Nor were these her only gifts. Once, in the early days, she covered the Sisters' expenses for a year while St John's House for Children was getting on its feet. She had inquired how much this would cost, and was told: 'Oh, more than anyone could afford. It comes to about seven thousand dollars.' Her casual reply was, 'I think I can manage that,' and she did.

Except for the garden where the Chapel of the Holy Child had been built, the hillside on which the 'small house at Arlington' stood was something of a wilderness. That did not last long. Fr Powell was blessed with a green thumb and an eye for the picturesque, so as the convent grounds expanded, the wilderness was transformed into a garden; several gardens, in fact, each with its own name and its own character. These scenic places—the Peace Rock, the Garden of Truth, 'Seldom Seen,' the Guardian Angel Rock—are lovingly described in a guidebook that Fr Powell wrote in 1923. Often he calls attention to particular trees and flowers. The loveliness of the natural world was for him what the Psalmist calls the 'beauty of holiness.' That is how he once explained the reason for 'high church' liturgy: 'God who lighted the stars in the sky probably likes to have shining candles in His church. He who embroidered the earth with crocuses and bluebells probably likes beautiful vestments to be used in His service. He who perfumed the sweet peas and the mignonette probably likes a sweet smell in church when His worship is being carried on.'

Bringing the Order of Saint Anne to birth is not the only work for which Fr Powell will be remembered. For a time he served as Superior of the American branch of the Society of St John the Evangelist, and he was a mentor and an inspiration to many, not least through the hundreds of letters he wrote. But in his own accounting, what he did for and with the Sisters surely came first. He asked to have his ashes buried in St Anne's Chapel, as close as they could be to where the Blessed Sacrament was reserved. In his last illness,

Father Powell and the Rule

It was far from being an academic treatise, or an arbitrary ultimatum, this rule; it grew like a living thing, and has become, as itself states, the skin of a living thought…Into it has gone the life-blood of our Father Founder, the fruit of his many years of experience, with the human soul in general, and the Religious Life in particular…While he was with us, one might almost say of him, as Louis the XIVth said of himself, "L'etat, c'est moi," 'The Rule, it is I,' since it was the expression and interpretation of his experience in the Religious Life, formulated for us.

Letter from Mother Ursula, OSA, written on hearing in China the news of Fr Powell's death

when the nursing he needed could not be given at the Mission House in Boston, he was taken to Arlington. 'You knew,' he said to the doctor, who had been an acolyte at St John's, 'that I wanted to die at home, didn't you?' January 12, 1938 was his seventy-third birthday. The next day he died. At the funeral, one of the pallbearers was Christopher McFadden, who nearly thirty years before had been the first baby that the Father Founder brought out to the new convent in Arlington.

Carving of the infant St John the Baptist

A sixteenth-century marble relief sculpture of the Madonna and Child on the west wall of St Anne's Chapel. It was placed in memory of Mother Anne, the first professed member of the Order to enter into rest.

A Child's Tribute

Father called us precious gems: that showed how much he liked us. He thought of himself last instead of first. He always wanted to give things, big or small, even if he had only a piece of string. Even after he was sick, he sent us candy with his love. I am sure that up in Heaven he is giving candy to the children, even if it is Heaven-candy...

Tribute from one of the children on the death of Fr Powell

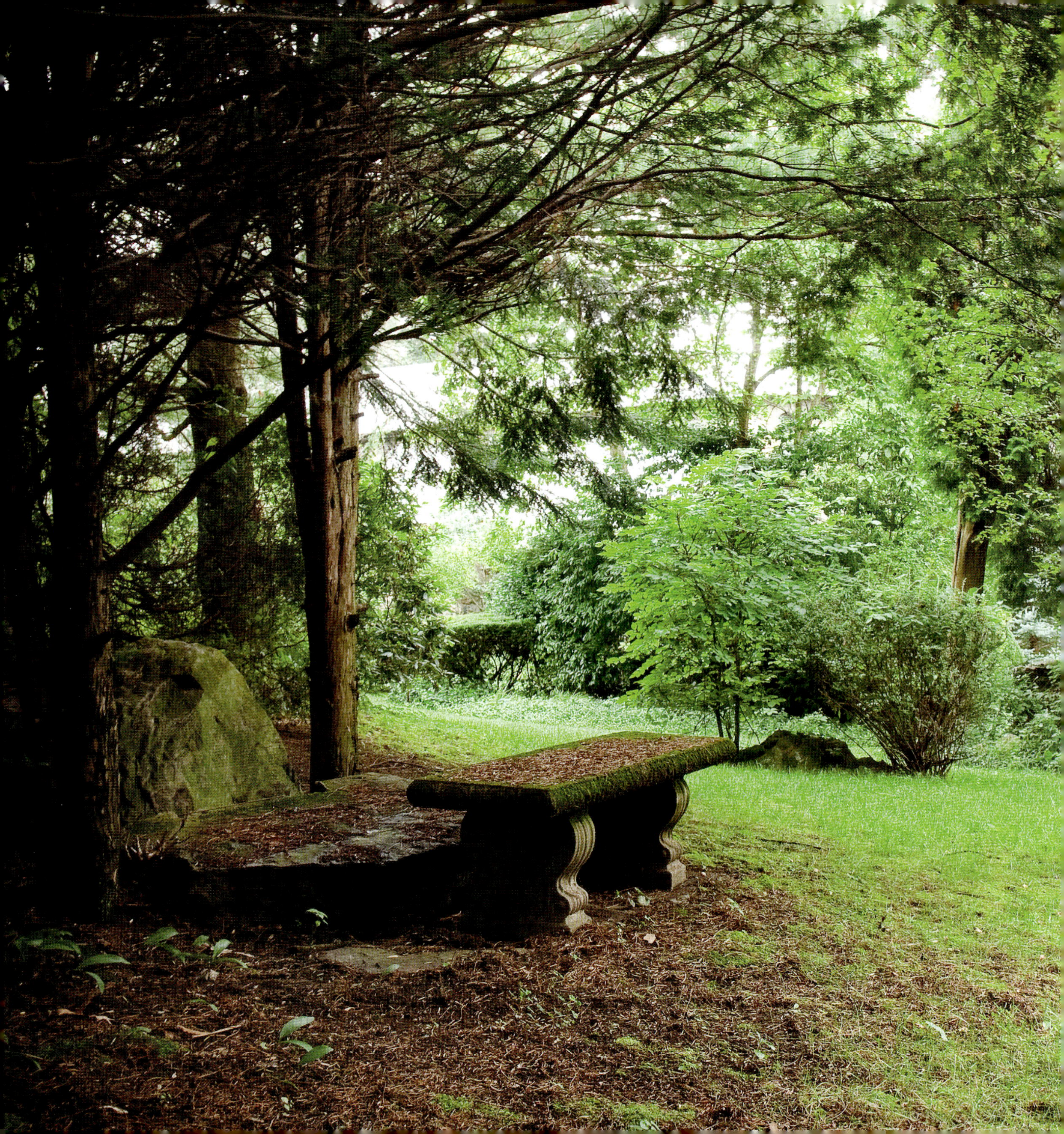

Interlude: Abundant, Gracious Hospitality

Be joyful in hope, persevere in hardship; keep praying regularly;
share with any of God's holy people who are in need; look for opportunities to be hospitable.
Romans 12:13

One thing that always has impressed me about the Sisters of Saint Anne, in addition to the devout lives they lead, is the ministry of abundant and gracious hospitality offered at their Bethany Convent. This is a sentiment shared by all who enter their house and chapel in Arlington, where a small community of women religious opens arms and hearts that seem wide enough to circle the globe.

Their welcome of friend and stranger to their hillside 'house' is so genuine as to make one feel that he or she is being greeted by family members who have been saving a space at table, just waiting for you to show up and take your rightful place. Many join me in expressing the feeling that they have prepared especially for you.

Despite their declining numbers over the years, these wonderful women, who probably never would refer to themselves as noble, have proved to be exactly that. Especially significant is the warmth and genuine affection expressed to all who attend their annual observance of St Anne's Day in late July. Joyous worship is followed by delicious food enjoyed on the beautiful convent grounds. The warmth and goodwill are contagious as guests, even strangers, engage with each other and genuinely enjoy what these gracious women offer to all.

Bishop Harris, who became the first woman bishop in the Anglican Communion in 1989, speaking in St Anne's Chapel at a Bethany House of Prayer Refreshment Day.

The warmth and love exuded by the Sisters are not limited to the confines of their convent. They enthusiastically join in celebrating occasions and events of significance in the lives of others—sometimes a life-profession of a member of another religious order, or a diocesan-wide program. Again, their joy and enthusiasm are palpable.

It is a privilege to salute these stalwart Sisters as they observe the hundredth anniversary of their founding—a joy to honor their ministry of hospitality and to pray God's richest blessings upon them and the work they do. They have been remolded and reshaped by God as time and circumstances have brought new dimensions to their life. With their 'Alongsiders' at the Bethany House of Prayer, the devoted Sisters of Saint Anne continue to live the words of the Apostle Paul's letter to the Romans—'share with any of God's holy people who are in need; look for opportunities to be hospitable.'

✠ Barbara C. Harris,
Bishop Suffragan of Massachusetts, *retired*

SAINT ANNE

GEMS
JULY

1920

Christus Natus Hodie

GEMS
December 1921

7 From Temple Street to Harvard Square

The three vows that every member of a religious order takes—poverty, celibate chastity, and obedience—imply an ordered way of life. With few exceptions, that life is lived within a community, but over the centuries it has taken a great many forms. What people are likely to associate with the idea of a 'nun' or a 'monk' has been different at different times. In the early 1900s, it was assumed that a woman in the religious life would wear what ladies wore in the Middle Ages, with a stiff, elaborate wimple enveloping her head. 'Taking the veil' meant becoming a nun. For nuns to dress in ordinary street-clothes was unheard of, as was the idea of their being employed in 'secular' work to support themselves. But the 'Second Order' Sisters of Saint Anne were ahead of their time. They did both.

THAT LITTLE WORLD BEHIND THE GATE

On Temple Street the people go
Past St. Anne's House, but few may know
That little world behind the gate
Where Sisters pray and work, till late.
(At least, until the clock strikes ten
P.M., you understand) and then
With Compline said, and lights put out,
With posture calm, and minds devout,
They sleep till sounds the rising bell
(Five-forty-five, the truth to tell).

Written for the thirtieth anniversary
of the Order of Saint Anne, 1940

The first plan was that women who adopted this new pattern of religious life would live in Arlington, together with the Sisters at St John's House, as one community. It was not a plan that commended itself to most of the Sisters. Quite the reverse. So instead another community was formed in Boston. Sister Angela, the one Sister who did favor the experiment, came there to take charge of it. She and her four Second Order companions, who were admitted as Postulants in March 1912, took up residence on Temple Street, in a house that was among the oldest in Boston and had seen some notable occupants in the past. Harriet Beecher Stowe is thought to have made her home there, and there Fr Richard Meux Benson, founder of the Society of St John the Evangelist, lived for a time. After serving as the Society's mission house, the building became a boarding house, and finally (after a large-scale clean-up) St Anne's House.

For forty years, St Anne's House was a spring from which many streams of ministry flowed. The Sisters shared it with the Church of St John the Evangelist, the Cowley Fathers' mission church, where they looked after the sacristy and were involved in social work and other parish activities. It was in the basement of St Anne's House that the Sisters themselves began to print GEMS, using a hand press purchased by Sister Louise, one of the original members of the Second Order. Named from the initials of the first three children at St John's House—Gertrude, Eva, and

Maude—these little booklets had begun to appear even before the first Sisters were clothed. For many years GEMS told friends and Associates of the Order about domestic events, mission activities, and the lives of the children. The Sisters looked forward to reading it too, as the illustrated poem 'To the Editor' attests. One purpose of GEMS was to ask for donations. During an especially difficult time, the Sisters sent out miniature coal bags, hoping that these would come back filled with cash to help pay for the heat.

From St Anne's House members of the Order were sent to Chicago, then to the Virgin Islands, then to Denver, and St Anne's House supplied the Sisters who worked among African-American children at St Augustine's Farm in Foxborough. Then, in 1952, the whole community was uprooted at once. City authorities discovered that the old buildings on Temple Street were not just old but dangerously decrepit. Ironically, there might not have been an inspection at all if St Anne's House had not been adjacent to St John's Church, where renovations had suddenly and dramatically become necessary. The story is told that one Sunday, after a long service, the Sisters who were on sacristy duty were still putting things in order when the time for dinner came. They left the church, as they usually did, by a door that led to the courtyard of St Anne's House. After dinner, Sister Natalie went back to finish her work. When she opened the door, 'she was almost strangled by a blast of what she took to be smoke. It was not smoke. There was no fire. It was thick dust mingled with grit. The entire ceiling of the church had caved in.'

JEWEL BOXES?

Elastic are our houses. We thought there wasn't a corner to spare, but find there is ample room for our Sisters from Boston, who were burned out of their Convent last week. Poor dears! but thank God no one was hurt. And what a delightfully large family it makes us! No wonder the police were a little mystified. A Sister, testifying as to the cause of the fire, kept repeating: 'And after the firemen emptied the closet, there were boxes and boxes of GEMS lying about the room ... .' We wonder they weren't accused in the newspapers of hoarding jewels.

'Memorabilia' in GEMS, September 1947

'The Patriarchs,' 44 and 46 Temple Street, built by Bela Clap about 1787. The Boston house of the Order of Saint Anne occupied number 44.

When it became clear that the Cowley Fathers could not afford to repair St Anne's House as well the church, the Sisters decided they would have to resign their work at St John's and leave Boston altogether. Fortunately, they had somewhere to go. Some years previously, they had purchased a three-story Victorian house near Harvard Square, where they rented rooms to young women studying at nearby Radcliffe College. So, after a short stay in Arlington, the Sisters from St Anne's House moved to Cambridge. Soon a two-car garage behind the house had been

The community of St Anne's House, on the steps of 44 Temple Street in 1913. At the back is Sister Angela, of the First Order; in front, wearing black, is Myra Kimball, then a Postulant, who became Sister Martha. Between them are Sisters Louise, Florence, and Mary Anne.

From Temple Street to Harvard Square

transformed into a simple chapel, St Joachim's, named for St Anne's husband. It was said to be the only garage in the world with stained-glass windows made by the famous Charles Connick. Between the chapel and the house, the Sisters built a small, utilitarian convent. The house itself became a guest house for older women who did not wish to live alone. At the same time, the Sisters added a cinderblock wing that could house a nursery school. The community from St Anne's House was resuming the mission for which their Order had been founded—nurturing children.

When St Anne's Play School opened in 1957, Mother Dorothy put Sister Natalie and Sister Judith in charge. They stayed at their post for thirty-five years. When they decided it was time to retire, friends planned a celebration for them, and the two Sisters were asked if they wanted children to come too. 'Without the children,' they answered, 'what fun would it be?' Some three hundred well-wishers attended the party, many of whom were once enrolled in the school. One of them, who had belonged to the original class of sixteen three-year-olds, wrote a winsome account of the day that was published in the New Yorker magazine. At the end of the article was a quip from Sister Natalie, a devoted fan of the Boston Red Sox. 'A man in the grocery store once said to me, "Sister, what do you think Heaven is like?" I said to him, "I really don't know, but if they have baseball there I'd be happy."'

A newspaper clipping from 1988 showing Sister Natalie as she throws out the first ball at a Boston Red Sox game.

The courtyard between St Anne's House and the Cowley Fathers' Mission Church of St John the Evangelist.

The guest house at 15 Craigie Street, Cambridge. Behind it stood the garage that became St Joachim's Chapel. In between were the convent and St Anne's Play School.

The Cambridge convent's next-door neighbor was the Buckingham Browne & Nichols School, with which the Sisters had cordial relations from the first. When the school bought their property in 1986, the Sisters were given tenancy for life—a 'handy agreement,' they thought. They continued to live in the convent, while the school used the house for meetings and turned the yard into a much-needed playground. In their retirement, the Sisters could still enjoy the sights and sounds of children playing outside the Refectory windows.

From Temple Street to Cambridge 53

Interlude: Nothing Showy

'Why don't you try Evening Prayer with the Sisters? Nothing showy. They simply pray.' That was my introduction to the Sisters of Saint Anne: a gentle suggestion made by Julia Slayton of Bethany House of Prayer. So off I went, grieving and lonely, to attend Evening Prayer—and enter another world. Only while at prayer with the Sisters was silence safe and tolerable. From that first day, the Sisters have offered me kindness, warmth, and a sense of the welcome Jesus himself would give. The honesty, quietness, and simplicity of their prayers are characteristic of the Sisters themselves. Now when I enter the Convent, as I often do, to enjoy a meal or work with the community, I cherish our time together and appreciate their care of me and of others. I see the talented, real individual in each Sister as well as their combined strengths. I recognize too the abiding history of past Sisters, whom I never met but whose words and actions inspire me. But through it all, the core of my understanding of the Sisters has continued to be anchored in the Office, their daily prayers. They do 'simply pray,' and that faithfulness in prayer not only centers their lives, but radiates to the lives of those around them as well.

Erica Gelser
Associate, Order of Saint Anne

The medal at the right is worn by Associates of the Order of Saint Anne.

Interlude: Coming Home

I know of no place where I feel God's welcoming and unconditional love more than when I am with the Sisters of Saint Anne, whether it be a liturgical service or simply sharing a meal. The hospitality they live by is one of infinite generosity and caring. Whenever I am at the convent, I feel as if I were 'coming home.' That is but one of the gifts they bestow, and always with an air of joy and delight. The Rule of Benedict says that the first step of humility is to 'keep the reverence of God always before our eyes'—and 'to see everything in life as sacred.' I know of no community where I feel this is as truly lived as it is with the Sisters of Saint Anne. My sense of gratitude and love for the Sisters knows no bounds. I feel as though I have been truly blessed, simply by being in their midst.

The Revd Eleanor Panasevich
Colleague in Ministry, Bethany House of Prayer,
and regular Eucharistic celebrant, St Anne's Chapel

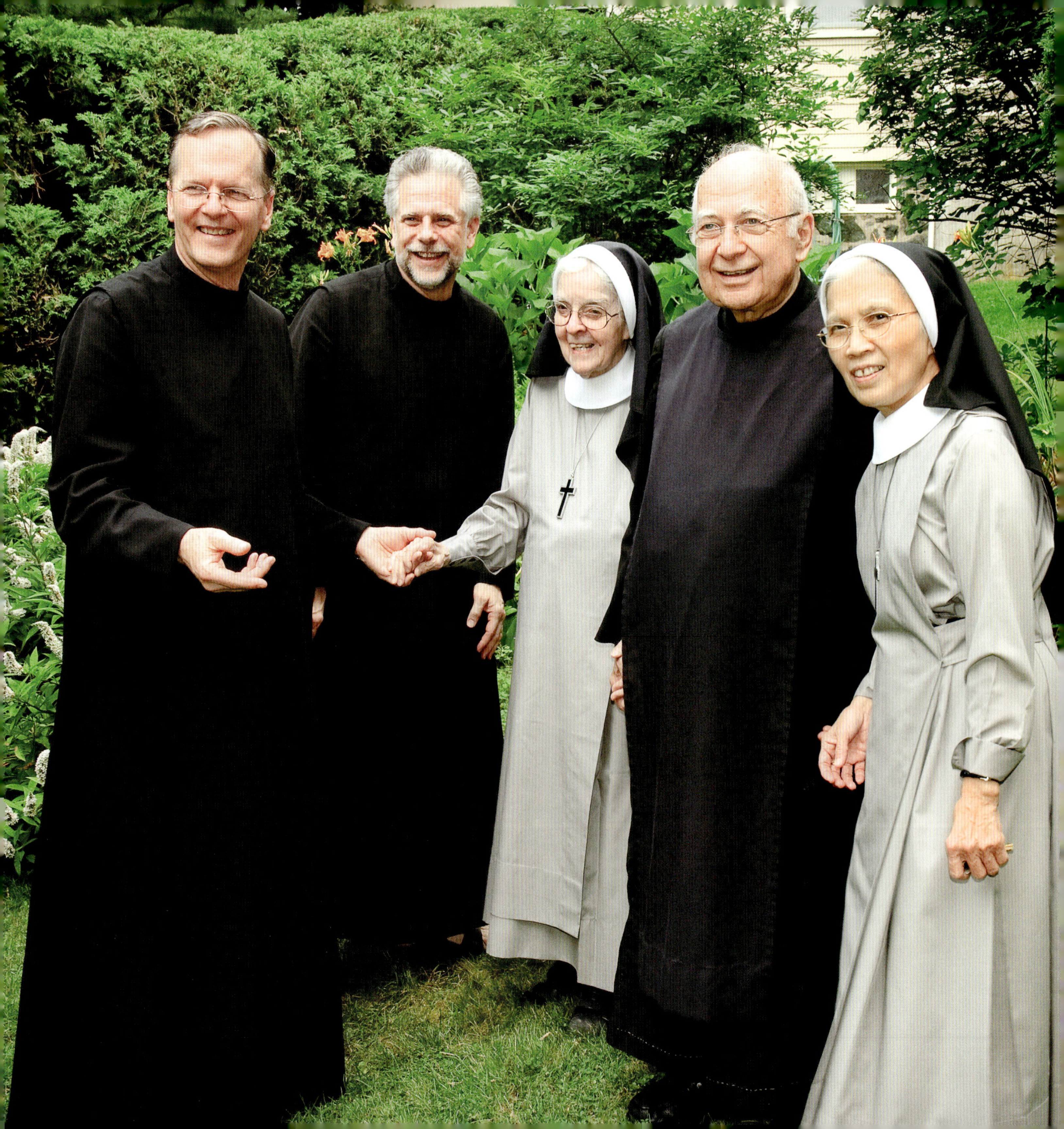

8 Foxborough

Between the Order of Saint Anne and the Society of Saint John the Evangelist there have always been close relations. No sooner had St Anne's House been established than some of the Sisters left Boston to take charge of the children at St Augustine's Farm, twenty-seven miles away, near what was then the village of Foxborough. At the turn of the century the Cowley Fathers had purchased the property, about 175 acres that included woods, lakes, and a cranberry bog, together with a farmhouse, barns, one hen, and a horse. There a convalescent home for African-American women and children had been founded by Fr Charles Field, SSJE, who was its chaplain for more than twenty years. When the Sisters arrived in 1914, it was Fr Field's custom to come to 'the Farm' from Boston every week, arriving on Monday and staying in a portable, prefabricated hut until the following Thursday. Another building of the same sort was being used for worship, but a permanent chapel, St Michael's, was under construction.

OPPOSITE: Brothers of the Society of Saint John the Evangelist with Sister Olga, OSA and Sister Maria Teresa, OSA on St Anne's Day, 2009: Curtis Almquist, SSJE (Superior), Jonathan Maury, SSJE and David Allen, SSJE.

A young visitor to the cemetery at 'The Farm' in Foxborough.

The children lived in the farmhouse. Behind it was a pond for swimming, and across the driveway a barn-like coach house, called the Playroom, for indoor romping. The facilities for the Sisters were minimal and the work prodigious. Hot water came from pots on the wood-stove in the kitchen, after it had been pumped by hand or drawn from a well. There were only kerosene lamps for lighting. Little by little, though, improvements began to be made. To double the capacity of the farmhouse, the Playroom was

Father Field

The real purpose of this paragraph is to tell about our deep love for the oldest Father in the Society. ... If in the days to come he should be old and feeble, unequal to the hard labour of the Farm, there will always be a warm corner for him by our kitchen fire—if he can get along with the Sisters. Of course, if he feels he'd be more independent doing a few light chores around the place, to sort of help pay for his board, we shouldn't want to stand in the way of his doing them; but we wouldn't ever require it of him, unless there was an extra rush of work. No, sir! You can bank on our gratitude to Father Field (there now, his name has popped out after all!) every time.

Gems, *March 1920*

moved and spliced on at the back as an annex, which was christened St Nicholas. A telephone line and running water were added. The Sisters became farmers in earnest, raising potatoes, radishes, parsnips, peas, and beans.

Between St Augustine's Farm and St Anne's House there were many comings and goings. For a time, the Novitiate of the Order was housed in Foxborough. Eventually it became clear that the Farm was not meeting expenses, and the convalescent work had to be discontinued. At about the same time, the Sisters were being called to new ministries beyond the Boston area—in the Virgin Islands and Chicago, then in Denver and Kingston. Their house in Foxborough came to an end, and the Farm has since been put to other uses. But in the cemetery there, side by side, are the graves of Sisters of the Order of Saint Anne, members of the Society of Saint John the Evangelist, and little children.

Some of the residents with some of the livestock.

St. Augustines children's Farm Foxboro, Mass.

Sisters and Gardens

There is not much time for the cultivation of individual gardens at the Farm. Life is so full of duties and chores. Nevertheless, as the summer advances, there will be gay showings of zinnias, petunias, marigolds, asters and other homely blossoms. Wherever they may have their abiding place, Sisters of St. Anne always have their gardens and they love them.

Sister Felicia Anne, OSA

Interlude: A Bond of Sweet Love

Father Charles Field of the Society of Saint John the Evangelist acquired property in Foxborough, Massachusetts, in 1898—Saint Augustine's Farm—to care for women of color from Boston who were suffering from chronic illness; frequently, tuberculosis. The Order of Saint Anne joined SSJE in this ministry. The property later developed into the Sisters' orphanage, and eventually into the Brothers' summer program for children-at-risk in Boston, Camp Saint Augustine. The Foxborough property holds many shared memories; the OSA and SSJE cemeteries adjoin one another there.

During the 1990s the Saint Anne's Sisters made a regular appearance during the summer camping season. The jovial Sister Gloria even spent some weeks in residence as a much-beloved staff member. In the summer of 1994, Sister Olga and I were speaking to the campers one afternoon during the daily chapel service. There we were, both dressed in our habits and both wearing a simple band on our ring fingers. Pointing to the rings, one of the young boys raised his hand and asked Sister Olga, 'Are you two married?' I guffawed; Sister Olga, never missing a beat, grabbed my arm, promptly placed a kiss on my cheek and said with a gleam in her eyes, 'No, but we love each other very much!' So true. Over these many decades, with the innumerable changes for both OSA and SSJE, the bond of sweet love between our two communities has remained a constant.

Sister Olga and Brother Curtis: 'We love each other very much!'

Two Superiors, St Anne's Day, 2009: Brother Curtis Almquist, SSJE and Sister Ana Clara, OSA.

The Revd Curtis G. Almquist, SSJE
Superior, Society of Saint John the Evangelist

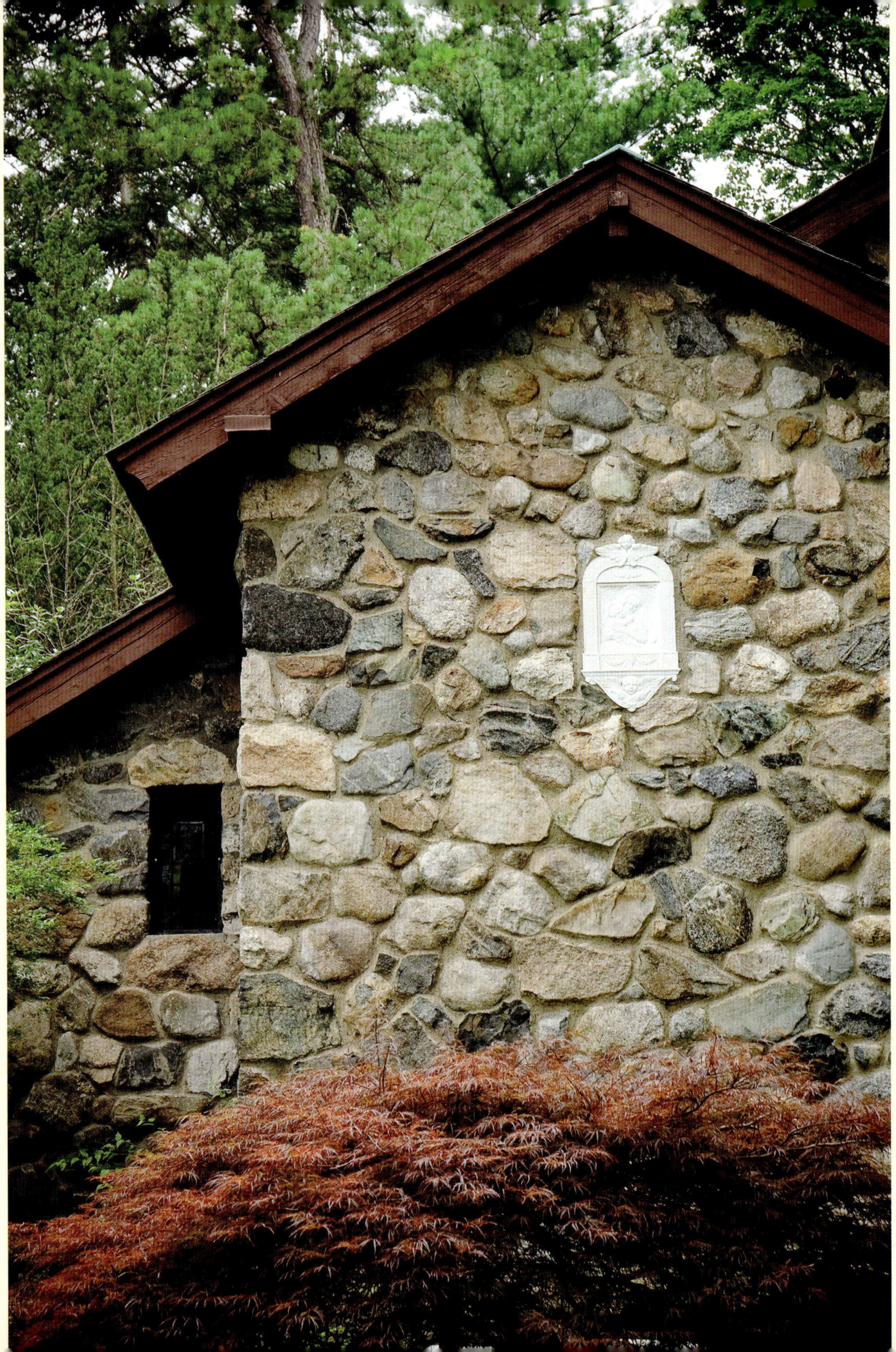

9 St Anne's Chapel

A religious community needs a place to pray together. Etheldred Barry turned a room in her house into a chapel for her Sunday School, and when that became too small a wooden chapel was built in what had been her garden. It was there, in the Chapel of the Holy Child, that the first Sisters of Saint Anne took their vows. But soon there were more Sisters, more children, more guests than this little building could hold, and it gave way to a new and much larger freestone chapel.

The stones, many of them, did not have far to travel. St Anne's Chapel, like the stone walls that have become a New England trademark, rose out of the rocky soil it stands on. Even before the professional builders arrived, the Sisters, their friends and Associates, the children—anyone who could dig—had gathered a pile of boulders ready to use.

Prayer for a New Chapel

O most blessed Lord and Saviour, Jesus Christ, Who didst say to Thine Apostles: suffer the little children to come to Me and forbid them not, we beseech Thee to enable us to build an house to Thy glory, where Thy children may worship Thee with reverence, and be taught in the faith of Thy Holy Catholic Church, Who livest and reignest, etc.

Collect composed in 1906 by Etheldred Breeze Barry, for the building of the Chapel of the Holy Child

Plans for the new chapel had been drawn up, as a gift to the Sisters, by the renowned ecclesiastical architect Ralph Adams Cram, who was then near the height of his career. All Saints Church in Ashmont, Massachusetts, was his work, and he had just been named architect of the Cathedral Church of St John the Divine in New York. He would later design the monastery chapel of the Society of Saint John the Evangelist in Cambridge. On the subject of what a church ought to look like, Cram had very definite ideas. Architecture, in his opinion, had taken a wrong turn at the Renaissance, and older buildings, either Gothic or Romanesque, were a better source of inspiration. Not that St Anne's Chapel copies any particular style directly or in detail. It does, however, evoke in a general way the architecture of the tenth or eleventh century. The original ground-plan was a simple rectangle, rounded into a semi-circle at the eastern end. On the south side was a porch. To the north, Mother Etheldred's wooden chapel was raised on jacks, given a quarter-turn, and attached so as to continue in use as a sacristy.

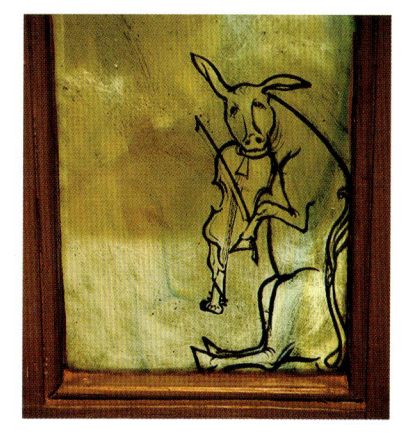

Inside, the stone walls were left unplastered and painted white. The high altar stood in the apse, and soon there was an elaborate Spanish reredos behind it.

An early photograph of the east end of the chapel, before the Chapel of the Holy Spirit was added, with the Father Founder, the Revd Frederick Cecil Powell SSJE, looking on.

Following a tradition nearly as old as monasticism, the stalls for the Sisters face each other along the north and south walls. The idea that 'form follows function' is exemplified in this arrangement, which is the architectural counterpart of the way worship has long been conducted in conventual chapels. Each of the services in the 'Divine Office,' from which the Anglican offices of Morning and Evening Prayer descend, includes Psalms, said or sung antiphonally—back and forth, that is, across the chapel, with half the 'choir' taking one verse and the other half the next. Parish churches often have stalls for singers arranged in the same way, but there is usually a much larger nave with forward-facing seats for the congregation. In St Anne's Chapel, which has never had parishioners to provide for, there is a nave of sorts, but a very short one. For the children, however, chairs could be brought in and placed close to the altar, between the Sisters' stalls.

Although its architecture was deliberately plain, the chapel was soon enriched with works of art and craft, many of them old and interesting. From Oxford came a gargoyle, from Stratford-upon-Avon a font, from a clipper ship the bell. Many of these antiquities were acquired and given to the Sisters by Frederick Cecil Powell, the Father Founder, who had this to say about them: 'The second-hand things are the big things; it is the second-hand things that matter. They've stood the test of time. That's one reason why we prefer a second-hand altar, a second-hand font, and second-hand pictures, and vestments, and stones in and about our Chapel. ... Certain things improve with long keeping and use.'

A few years later, readers of GEMS were told, 'The time has come for enlarging the Chapel. Like the sons of the prophets, under Elisha, the place where we worship and dwell "is too strait for us." We need a larger playroom and dormitory and refectory and chapel. But the Chapel must come first.' Enlargement took the form of a side chapel on the south, dedicated to the Holy Spirit. There the Blessed Sacrament is reserved, and there Fr Powell's ashes are buried. To the north, a new stone sacristy replaced what had been the Order's first chapel. Inside, at one end of the chapel, there was once a rood-beam, supporting a crucifix flanked by figures of St Mary and St John, which has been removed; at the other end, a gallery was added. What was once the entrance-porch is now a tiny Lady Chapel, dedicated to the Virgin Mary, St Anne's daughter.

In keeping with liturgical change that began in the 1960s, a freestanding altar replaced the baroque high altar, with its tabernacle and six tall candlesticks. One attempt to fill the space on the east wall was an image of Christ crucified, without a cross. Another, even more striking, was the face of the Man of Sorrows, sculpted in metal. These gave way to the more traditional crucifix that appears in the apse today.

St Anne's Chapel 63

More noticeable changes came later, when the apse was re-ordered to accommodate new liturgical practices—which in fact are very old—that began to be introduced towards the end of the twentieth century. By and large, Anglo-Catholic worship had tended to conform with Roman Catholic practice, apart from the language in which it was conducted. But after the Second Vatican Council, Roman Catholics themselves

An early photograph of the west end of the chapel.

set aside many of these old ways—which in fact were not all that old—in favor of reforms that had long been advocated by the Liturgical Movement, as it is called. The most conspicuous of these changes affected the position of the celebrant and other ministers at Mass. Instead of facing east for most of the service, they moved to the other side of the altar so as to face the congregation. Although adopting this practice usually meant moving the altar, Anglicans for the most part welcomed it, and today it is the rule rather than the exception in the Episcopal Church. For St Anne's Chapel a new, free-standing altar was built, with plenty of space behind it for the Eucharistic ministers.

The Chapel of the Holy Spirit, as it appeared shortly after it was built on the south side of St Anne's Chapel. The border and the calligraphic text are the work of Mother Etheldred.

64 ∞ Catch the Vision

Interlude: A Different Kind of Space

Many friends and Associates of the Order of Saint Anne will remember their first visit to the chapel at Arlington. To get there, most of us drive on expressways, dodging traffic, passing shopping malls, then winding past secure, isolated neighborhood homes. To arrive and walk inside the chapel, however, is to enter a different kind of space, ordered not by expediency or economics or human competitive display, but by a curious and wonderful embodiment of what the founders and their successors sought by forming and being a monastic community.

The chapel calls the person entering it into a stillness, even a sense of awe, yet does so without intimidation or exclusion. To enter is to belong, if only for those moments—but those moments have eternal significance. The high white interior walls give a sense of benignly enclosing everyone within. The arrangement of its interior in the 'choir' evokes a sense of community and peace rarely found otherwise.

The intriguing assembly of ancient objects—a plaque here, a column there, a piece of glass, a stone—is a treasure trove which does not distract from the overall simplicity of the place, and yet suggests that there will always be new discoveries there, and that only over many years, if ever, could one really know every nook and cranny.

My own experience of the Order is centered on this space, and on liturgy and prayer shared with those whose home it more permanently is. The space itself is a sign of the community there: of the peace and warmth that the community of the Sisters of Saint Anne offers freely to others, and also of the more varied forms of community created there in those eternal moments of prayer and sacrament.

In 1998 I was invited to assist at a weekly Eucharist, of which the celebration soon became a regular duty and privilege. Recently, after a return visit, it occurred to me that I have never felt more peaceful or more grounded in liturgy than in that place, and with those who gathered there to pray, to remember Jesus, to break bread, and to sing praise. This has been a great gift to me from the Sisters, who are themselves a gift from God to so many of their friends. Although distant now physically, my membership as a Priest Associate of the Order is a happy and lasting connection with a place and with people for whom I am deeply grateful.

The Revd Andrew McGowan
Warden, Trinity College,
The University of Melbourne

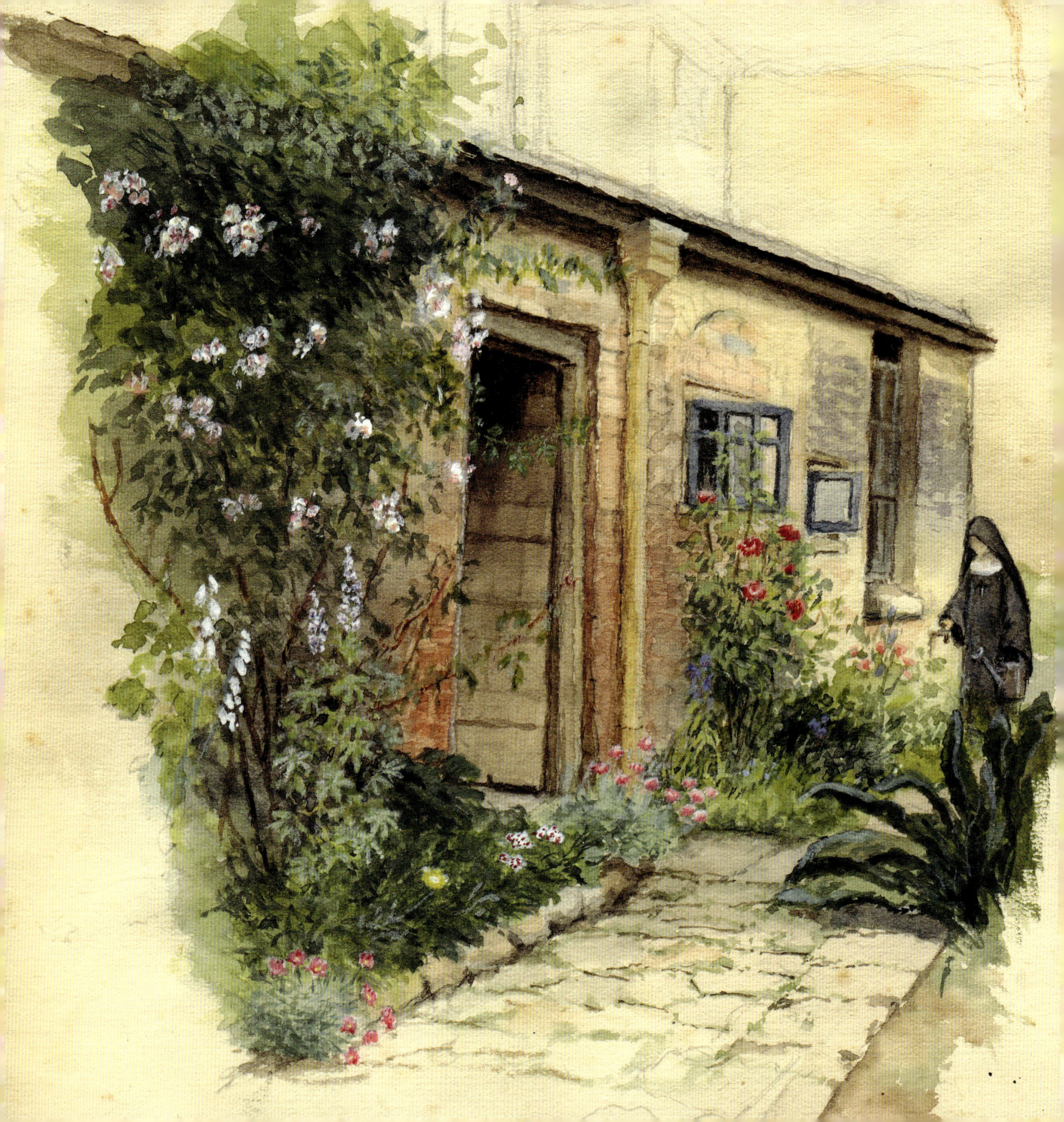

10 England, the Fourth Foundation

By 1917 there were three houses of the Order of Saint Anne, two in Massachusetts and one in China. The fourth was to be founded, as the first had been, by Mother Etheldred. Less than a year after she was professed in life vows, she was installed as Mother of a new convent, and together with three other members of the Order, who themselves were English, she set out for England to make that convent a reality.

The idea of planting an American religious order in England—the reverse of what usually happened—was conceived by the indefatigable Fr Powell. The Order of Saint Anne was already known to two of his aristocratic English friends, Lady Henry Somerset and her sister Adeline, Dowager Duchess of Bedford, both of whom had visited St John's House and were Associates of the Order. Lady Henry was the mainstay of the Duxhurst Colony, a little village of thatched cottages near Reigate in Surrey, which had been established for rehabilitating women addicted to drink. By the beginning of the Great War, as it was then called, Duxhurst was also caring for orphans and deserted babies, as well as for girls sent there by civil authorities as first-offense cases. Lady Henry decided that the Colony should be entirely devoted to working with young children, and hoped to put a religious community in charge. That community, at Fr Powell's suggestion, was the Order of Saint Anne.

In more ways than one, the four Sisters who sailed for England in 1917 were setting out on a venture of faith. Because of the war, their ship had its portholes blacked out, and the threat of being attacked by submarines was real. There were few passengers, but among the few was a bishop returning from Australia, who celebrated Mass on an improvised altar in the saloon, though only after the mermaids painted on the walls had been covered up.

The voyage was rough but otherwise uneventful. As soon as Lady Henry had obtained permission from the Archbishop of Canterbury, the new convent was formally established at Duxhurst. It did not take long to discover that finances there were precarious. The local grocer refused to make further deliveries until his bill was paid. Mother Etheldred promptly began to take in paying guests, as she had done in the early days at Arlington. Later, on finding that Duxhurst was built on clay that could be modeled and fired, she had a kiln built, and presently jugs and casseroles were being sold to help pay the bills. Some of these wares were shipped to Boston, where they were advertized in GEMS, the Order's magazine, with the help of a poem about 'the Duxhurst Duck.'

The community grew, but so did the Colony's debts. 'Her Ladyship!' the Secretary had said to Mother Etheldred. 'I know she is a saint, but she has no idea of money matters.' Unfortunately, he was right. When Lady Henry died in 1921, a year after her sister the Duchess, there was nothing to be done except close down the work at Duxhurst. For the Sisters there were

OPPOSITE: A watercolor sketch, dated 1942 and thought to have been painted by Mother Etheldred, showing the Sisters' garden at the Emsworth convent.

various possibilities. They could disperse to other convents, return to America, or remain in England and find a new home. They chose to stay, and stay together. For a time they were in charge of a retreat house near Portsmouth, on the south coast of England. Eventually they settled in a larger house not far away at Emsworth, close to Chichester Theological College. When the time came to move in, the other Sisters traveled by bus, but Mother Etheldred went in a taxicab, taking their most important possessions with her—a chalice and paten, two valuable crucifixes, the convent's pet goldfinch, and a large medieval statue of St Anne. The statue, she reports, 'occupied the outside seat beside the driver, to the great amusement of the people we met.'

Devoted though she was to the Order's work with children, Mother Etheldred had always longed for the 'enclosed' life of the contemplative religious orders, separated from the secular world. When the community had been at Duxhurst for more than a year, the priest who was acting as their chaplain said to her, 'very seriously' as she recalls, 'Reverend Mother, if you feel God calls you to the contemplative life, you must live it, even if you have to leave your Order.' That is what she certainly did feel, yet at the same time she was convinced that such a life could be lived in the Order of Saint Anne. 'Our Holy Rule provided for it.' At Emsworth the Sisters could finally 'keep enclosure,' and they did. It helped that their chapel was close to the College. Priests on the faculty came to celebrate Mass, bringing with them students to serve as acolytes. When business outside the convent had to be done, the Sisters could call on Miss Penfold, who lived as a solitary in a caravan on the grounds, worked in the garden, and used her bicycle to 'go errands.'

The character of the religious life, especially in its contemplative form, does not lend itself to colorful narrative. If anything, it is meant to do just the opposite. It is a life that draws its strength from the daily round of prayer, varying a little with the seasons of the Church year, but otherwise keeping up a steady, quiet rhythm that stands in sharp contrast with the hectic way in which much of the world is apt to run. So it was at Emsworth. The Sisters prayed. They provided space and time for retreats. After a while they acquired a nearby house, to serve as a presbytery for their chaplain, and added a wing to their convent. Mother Etheldred served the two terms of office which the Rule then allowed. She lived to see the fiftieth anniversary of the Order she had done so much to found. By then its four convents had become eight, and many things had changed. '*What* are you *wearing*?' she exclaimed, when one of the American Sisters called, dressed in the new, shorter habit her convent had adopted. In 1967, half a century after setting out for England, Mother Etheldred died at the age of ninety-seven.

'ANYTHING YOU CAN SEND'

Please pray for us and for this very real venture of faith. We have almost no income to depend upon, and not an article of furniture for our two houses. We shall need beds, bedding, chairs, toilet sets, table ware, and cooking utensils. Anything you can send us, from a bedstead to a scrubbing brush, will be most gladly welcomed. …

Above all, give us your prayers, that through our House of Retreat many may come to know God, not merely to know about Him.

Letter sent to Associates by Mother Etheldred, OSA, as the community was leaving Duxhurst, summer 1921

Watercolors, perhaps Mother Etheldred's work, showing the kitchen at Emsworth (with the convent cat) and a Sister ringing the bell for worship.

The medieval statue of St Anne that made the trip to Emsworth by taxicab.

Mother Etheldred in her later years.

One of the thatched cottages that made up the 'village' at Duxhurst.

England, the Fourth Foundation ⁘ **69**

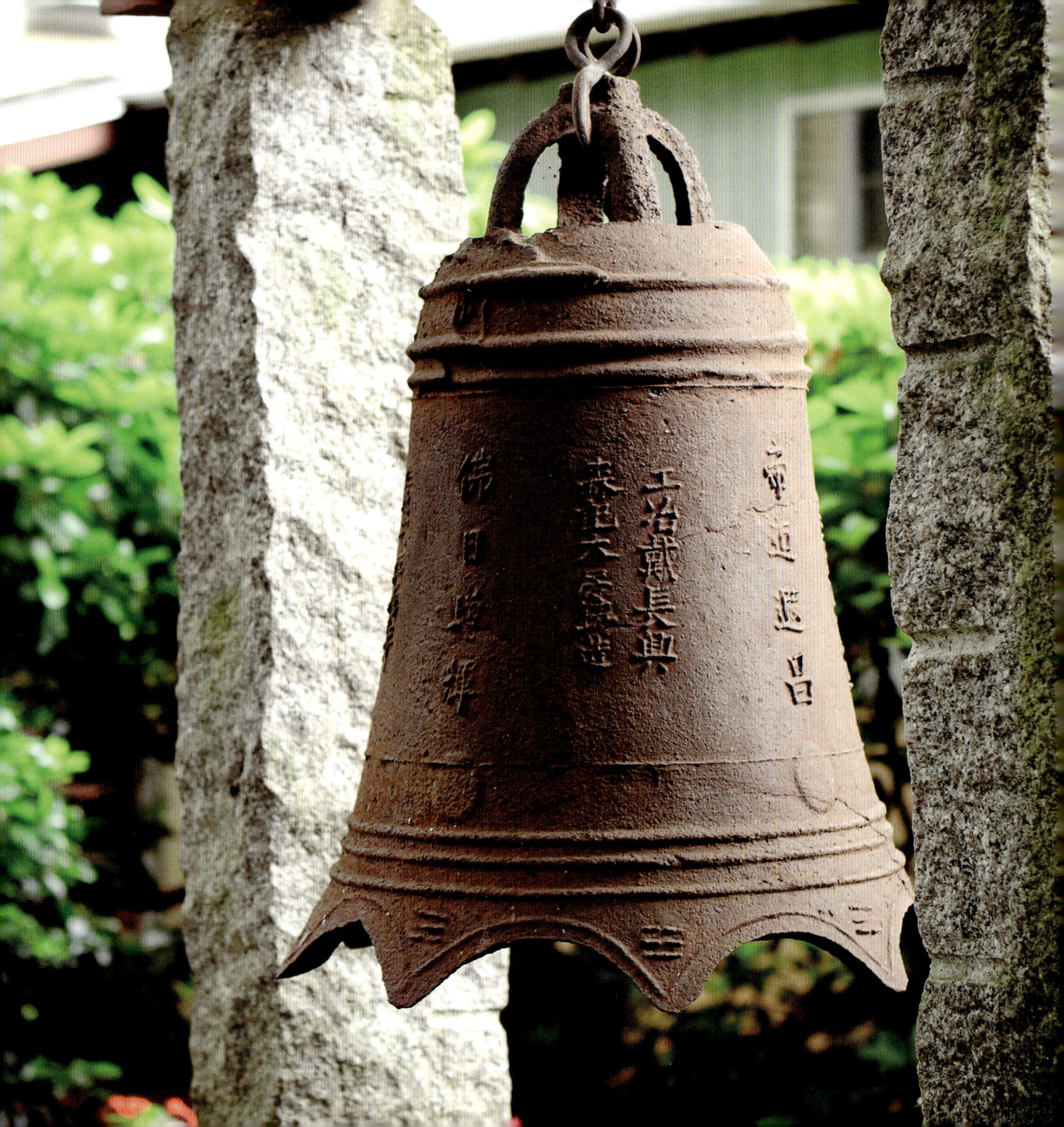
帝道遐昌
佛日增輝

11 China

'A missionary vocation was almost the last thing the Sisters of Saint Anne thought of as being possible for themselves.' So they said in the guide book that the Order published in 1923. 'We longed to do the will of God, and to dedicate ourselves afresh to him, while we ministered to the needs of a few children in America, and lo! he has called us to far distant lands.'

The first land they were called to could not have been much farther distant. It was China. The call to go there came at the hands of Fr Robert Wood, who was priest-in-charge of St Michael and All Angels Church in Wuchang, now one of the 'Three Towns of Wuhan' on the Chang Jiang (Yangtse) River in south-central China. Fr Wood had visited the convent in Arlington shortly after it was founded. With him came a missionary nurse from Wuchang, who was a member of St John's Church in Boston. With their encouragement, and the blessing of the Episcopal Church's Board of Missions, the Order of Saint Anne elected Sister Ursula as Mother and sent her with three other Sisters to China.

Fr Wood had been living in a house originally built as a residence for several clergy. When the Sisters arrived, he turned it over to them as their convent, and found lodging elsewhere. By January 1917 the community was settling in. 'Whatever you do,' Mother Ursula wrote, 'don't come to China in winter!' It was an unusually severe winter. Little boys who worked in the factories were brought to St Michael's, where the Sisters gave them a hot meal and found them something to keep their hands and feet warm. As for themselves, every layer of clothing the Sisters could put on they did. The result, Mother Ursula reported, was that 'you would never recognize such corpulent beings as your slender Sisters. Sister Margaret is almost as broad as she is long now.'

Winter passed, and by the time of the Order's patronal festival on October 2, the feast of the Holy Guardian Angels, the first postulant, Sister Anita, was admitted. She was the niece of one Bishop in China and

OPPOSITE: The Chinese bell sent to Arlington by the Sisters in China, and dedicated on St Anne's Day in 1930. It is believed to date from 1368, the second year of the Ming Dynasty, which according to the prophecy inscribed on the bell will last forever.

DOING WHAT IS AT HAND

I do believe, too that God sent us here, and that our sacrifice and yours will be fruitful, though none of us may see the fruit in this world. That is why I felt we must try to go on, and this last return to China was the hardest thing I have ever done, I can assure you. It would have been so easy to give up, but I could not believe it was right. And as we go on day by day, seeing nothing of the future, but doing what there is at hand, not seeming to accomplish much, no permanent abiding place, yet, still one feels that God is leading us and that is what He wants. At any rate it is a sacrifice, and real sacrifice must bear fruit in some way.

Mother Ursula, OSA—letter to her mother from China, March 1929

the granddaughter of another. Not long afterwards, a newborn infant, abandoned, as were many baby girls, was baptized and taken to Wuchang to be the first Chinese child at the convent. Mission work in China included religious instruction, which had to be given in Chinese. Sister Augusta, who worked for several years at Wuchang, spent five hours a day with a Chinese tutor, followed by two or three hours on her own. After a year of this formidable program, she could compose a Bible story, translate it into Chinese, and memorize it. While this was no small accomplishment, it still left one of the children puzzled. 'The foreign Sister can tell us stories and sing songs, but she can't talk to us.' In time she could do that too, though it was never easy. Even Sister Anita, whose Chinese was otherwise fluent, had difficulty, chiefly because the meaning of a Chinese syllable is not determined only by the sound of its vowels and consonants. The same word can have different meanings when it is said at different pitches. Sister Anita once told what she thought was a story about Jesus casting out an evil spirit, only to learn that what she had said was that he cast out a turtle.

With the outbreak of full-scale war between China and Japan in 1937, the Sisters' situation became precarious. Their convent was bombed. No one was seriously hurt, and the community moved into Bishop Gilman's house in the Cathedral compound, across the river in Hankow. For a time they kept up their work, but in 1941 the Bishop had to ask everyone in the mission to leave China. The Sisters went to the Philippine Islands, and the Bishop there put them in charge of a boarding school in the city of Baguio. When the Sino-Japanese War merged into the larger conflict of World War II

Sister Helena

I and all my family had always been Buddhists but after my association with the Sisters, I became interested in Christianity and had the desire to become a nun. Sister Anita gave me instructions and prepared me for Baptism and Confirmation. I was confirmed by Bishop Gilman, and soon after began my Postulancy for the Religious Life. In 1938 I was clothed as a Novice in the Order of St Anne and given the name Helena.

Two months later, the war with Japan began. My parents became alarmed at the idea of our family being separated from each other under these conditions and sent my brother from Han Chuan, 180 miles by Han River, to take me home. I stayed in hiding with my parents in the country for six months. Then I received word from Mother Ursula saying it seemed safe to return to the Convent. The journey itself seemed very dangerous to us, however, with so many Japanese soldiers about. My brother thought it best that I dress in boy's clothes, which I did, and he and I arrived safely at the Convent on Christmas Day, or rather at the compound across the river in Hankow. For while I was at home, the Convent on St Michael's compound had been hit by a Japanese bomb, and destroyed.

from a narrative of her life in religion written by Sister Helena, OSA

and Japanese occupation of the Philippines began, the Sisters were first forced to leave the city, and then to return—as internees, with six hundred others, in a concentration camp.

Camp Holmes was the Sisters' home for three years and a half. They lived in one of three huts on 'Nunnery Row,' with Roman Maryknoll Sisters and Sisters of St Mary as neighbors. 'We were able to carry

Anne Wu, the first child cared for by the 'China Sisters.' This photograph, taken in 1919, shows her with Sister Joan, Mother Ursula, and Sister Margaret.

Two unidentified photographs from the convent at Wuchang.

China ✤ 73

Internment

Fortunately we did not know what a narrow escape we had from a fate that has overtaken other civilian camps where the prisoners were ruthlessly massacred. I wish you could see this funny old place—once used as a prison and condemned for even that purpose and partially demolished—we have been grateful enough for the high and solid walls which have protected us from fire and shooting.

Letter from Mother Ursula, OSA, in Camp Holmes, to Mother Miriam, OSA, March 8, 1945

on convent life fairly well,' Sister Augusta later wrote, 'though eating, sleeping, saying Offices, and bathing, all in one small room, required some dove-tailing.' There were doctors, dentists, and nurses in the camp, as well as eight priests and a bishop. Mass was said every day, and sung on great festivals. There were a hundred children too, and although books were few there was a school.

At the end of 1944, when American troops were converging on the Philippines, the whole camp was evacuated to the Bilibid Prison in Manila, along with former defenders of Bataan and Corregidor. The city was recaptured by General Douglas MacArthur, whom Sister Augusta was the first to greet when he appeared at the prison in person. Later, when she had at last returned to the United States, she found herself giving information to a clerk. It was a routine bureaucratic inquiry about name, age, and so on, until it came to the question, 'Have you ever been in prison?' 'Yes,' said Sister Augusta, quite truthfully. When the astonished clerk looked up and asked, 'How long?' she anticipated his next question. 'About two months and a half. A prisoner of war.'

When the Sisters returned to China in 1946, World War II was over, but civil war between Nationalists and Communists had resumed. Only one of the buildings used by the church in Wuchang was left standing. At Hankow, however, the 'China Sisters' were able to re-establish St Anne's Kindergarten. As before, they had to rely on their Sisters in America, Mother Miriam especially, to send them things they could not find in China—linens, shoes, a stove, and even an organ—as well as food. Altar bread too had to come in parcels from America. To ensure a regular supply, the Sisters decided they would have to bake it themselves, and a letter went off to Arlington, asking for one electric altar-bread baker, one transformer, and two bread cutters. Mother Miriam, who was used to such requests, was as vexed as anyone to learn that when the package arrived in China, nearly a year later, the equipment she had sent was damaged. 'To think that after all we went through,' she wrote to Mother Ursula, 'you cannot use it!' Repairs and rewiring helped, but not much. If the electric baker did not scorch the hosts, they stuck to it.

Outside the convent there were more serious difficulties to deal with. The People's Republic of China had been proclaimed by Mao Zedong, and all religious teaching was suspect. By 1950 the new Bishop was urging the Sisters to leave once again. Five of them, including Mother Ursula and Sister Anita, returned to the Philippines. 'We seem to be a sort of Religious Migrants,' Mother Ursula wrote, 'but we hope some day to stay put in Heavenly Mansions!' In the meantime they continued their mission work at St Francis's Mission in Upi. And that is another story.

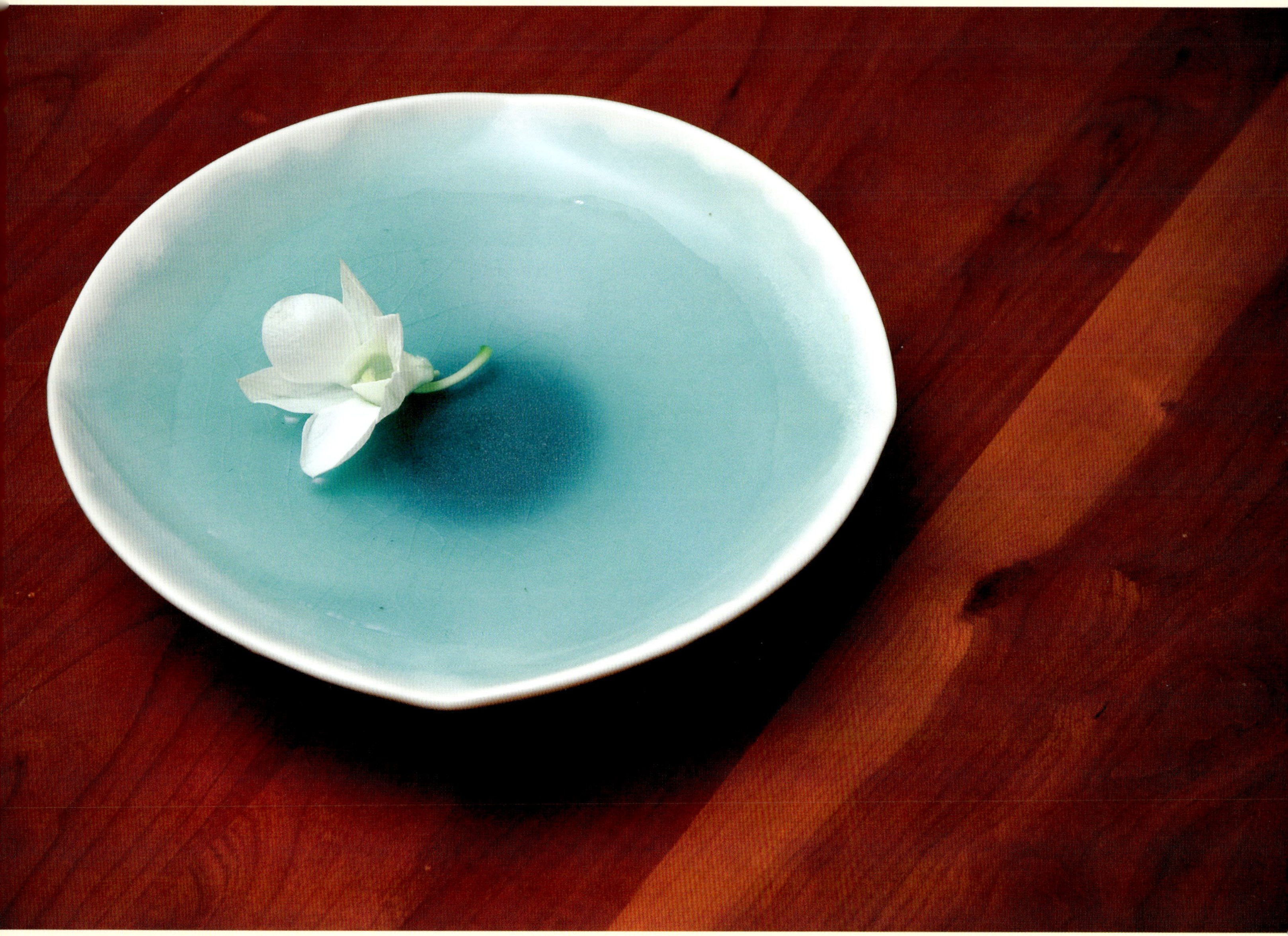

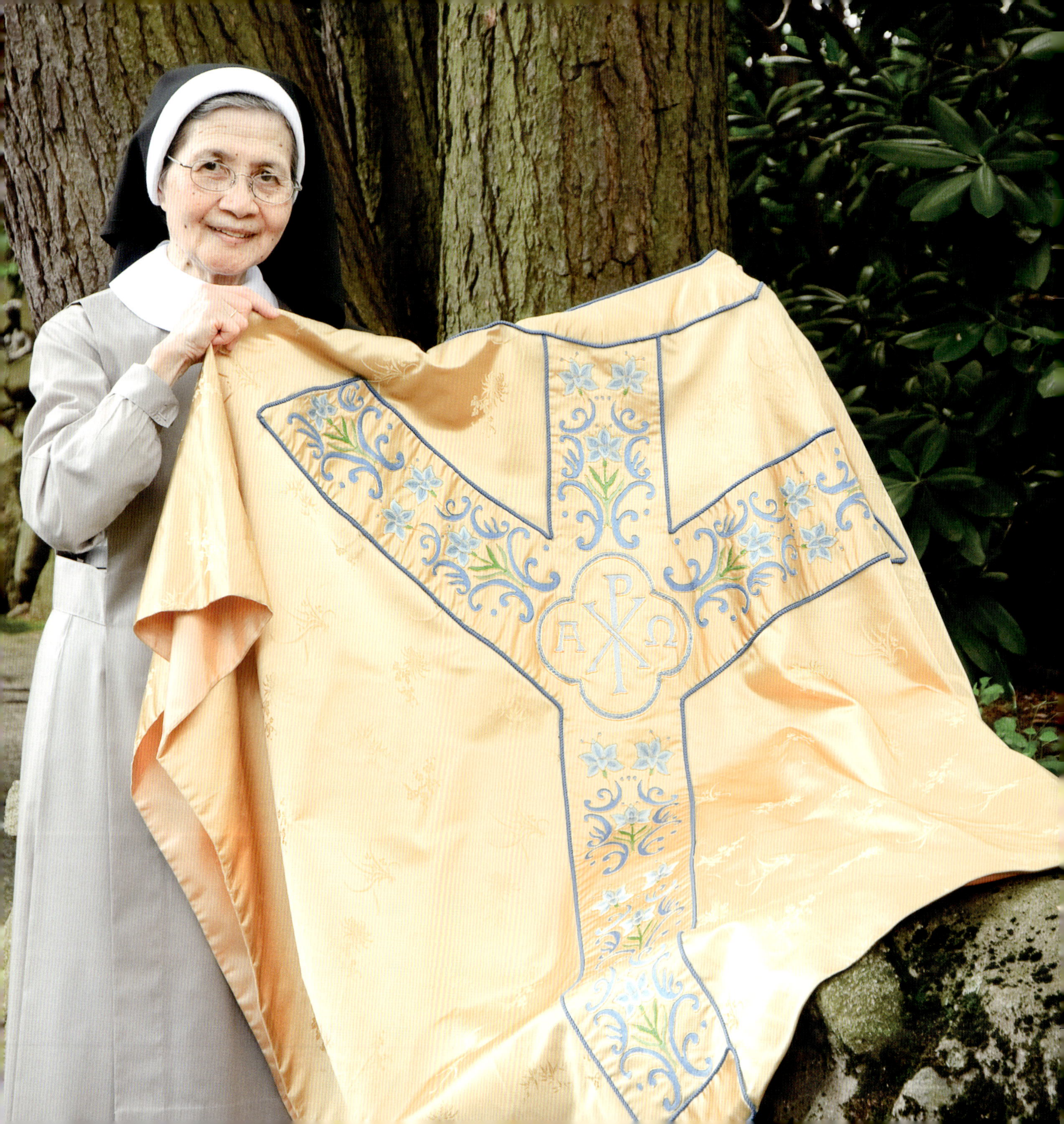

12 The Philippines

When the Order of Saint Anne came to the Philippines in 1951, the Sisters were no strangers. Ten years before, when the whole community at the convent in China had been asked to leave because of the Sino-Japanese War, the new Bishop of the Philippine Episcopal Church, Norman Spencer Binsted, invited the Sisters to assume a role at the Easter School in Baguio on the northern Philippine island of Luzon. After World War II had ended, they went back to China, but found the country torn by its own civil war, which led to the establishment of a Communist state that did not welcome Christian missionary efforts. When it became clear that they would have to migrate once again, the Sisters asked Bishop Binsted if they might come back to the Philippines. His reply was a cordial invitation, and back they came.

The war had devastated nearly all the institutions of the church, especially in the north. Instead of returning to Luzon, the Sisters went to the small town of Upi in the Cotabato province on the southern island of Mindanao. Missionary work among the semi-nomadic Tiruray people had begun in Cotabato early in the 1920s. In 1927 Upi became its headquarters and the Mission of St Francis of Assisi was opened. Besides the central mission station at Upi, there were several outstations in the surrounding hills. Most of these could be reached only by hiking or on horseback. In the rainy season, people who came to church sometimes brought an extra set of dry clothes, knowing they would have to wade through swollen streams along the way.

In Upi the Sisters took up the kinds of ministry that had been theirs in China—evangelism, teaching, altar guild work, advising the very active Women's Auxiliary. Although fabrics and other materials were often hard to get, a 'vestment department' was re-established. Beautifully embroidered copes, stoles, chasubles, and even an occasional miter were sent to churches in the Philippines and beyond. The Sisters cared for a dormitory, where girls lived while studying at the Upi Agricultural High School, about a mile away. Meanwhile,

OPPOSITE: Sister Maria Agnes, OSA displaying the festal chasuble she helped to embroider at the convent in Upi. It belongs to a set of vestments still in use at the convent in Arlington.

CHRISTMAS AT UPI

And so we come to Christmas, sans snow, sans holly and tapering evergreen trees, but gay with poinsettias from our own garden, vocal with the chirp of crickets, and deep bass of frogs, and the clucking of little lizards, all taking their part in the great orchestra of Nature, welcoming her Lord with the ox and ass, and men and angels. Yes, we do have angels even here in Upi, and very close to us they are, away from the madding crowd of men, in the great silences of the hills under a wide expanse of sky.

Letter from Mother Ursula, OSA, from the Philippine Islands convent, 1956

'at the other end of the educational process,' as Mother Ursula put it in a diocesan paper, there was once again a kindergarten to supervise. She added that despite a policy stating how old children had to be before they were admitted, 'some have almost literally crept in at the tender age of two.'

It was Bishop Binsted's conviction that a strong native ministry was essential to the mission's flourishing. The same ideal applied to religious orders. Soon after coming to Upi, the Sisters received their first Filipina postulant, Sister Gloriana, and another arrived shortly after that. Even with these new recruits, however, it was becoming more and more difficult to maintain the convent's life and work. As Mother Ursula pointed out again and again to Mother Miriam in Arlington, the Sisters who had come to the Philippines from China were getting no younger. The Warden of their convent agreed that its work could continue only if a younger Sister—or better, two—could be sent from America. So it was that in 1961 Mother Miriam made her second trip to Upi, bringing with her Sister Olga. A year later, Mother Ursula, who had been present fifty years before, when the first Sisters of Saint Anne entered the Order, returned to the convent in Arlington from which she had set out for the Far East.

The convent in Upi became a branch house, with Sister Olga—Sister Maria Dolorosa, as she was then known—in charge. To the girls living in Angel House at the convent in Kingston, New York, she wrote a moving letter describing what the words 'I go to school every day' would have meant for most girls and boys in that part of the Philippines. It would have meant walking through tall, wet grass, carrying rice for lunch, wrapped in a banana leaf, to arrive at a flimsily-built schoolhouse where there were no books and everything had to be learned by rote. It would have meant coming home to a house with one improvised kerosene lamp, and sleeping on a grass mat. Writing in the voice of such a child, Sister Olga continues: 'Now you can begin to know my joy in living in the Mission Dormitory, and attending the Mission High School'—a galvanized iron roof overhead, a change of clothes, a sweater, a towel. 'We have spoons and pressure lanterns and dictionaries and maps and a globe.' The letter concludes with the hope that 'through education, love, and interest, some will be raised up to improve the lot of the Tiruray people.'

As the 1960s went on the political and religious situation in Cotabato became more and more unsettled and potentially hazardous for Christian missionary work. Yet another move seemed prudent. Plans were made to transfer the Sisters' work to Manila, where most of the Episcopal Church's activity was concentrated. Meanwhile, in America, the Order of Saint Anne was embarking on a new ministry in Lincoln, Massachusetts—Bethany, a residential center of care for women with developmental disabilities. The Sisters in the Philippines decided that they would stay together as a community, and relocate in Lincoln, there to join in prayer and work with Sisters from Arlington and the Kingston convent as the youngest house of the Order of Saint Anne.

Sister Olga and Mother Miriam in the Deer Park at Nara, Japan, where they stopped on their way to the Philippines.

Mother Ursula and Sister Anita, going to market.

The Philippines convent: from left to right, Sisters Maria Teresa, Gloriana, Maria Agnes, and Olga, Mrs Millan, Sister Ana Clara, and Danillo Millan.

Sister Ana Clara and Sister Maria Agnes assisting at the consecration of
the Rt Revd James Manguramas as Bishop of the Diocese of Southern
Philippines, September 14, 1993. Bishop James's older brother
Constancio had been Bishop of the same diocese.

The interior of the Mission Church of St Francis of Assisi at Upi.

Interlude: Remembering Upi

First, my congratulations to the Sisters of Saint Anne on the hundredth anniversary of their Order, and for their hundred years of spiritual life and service to God and his church. May he continue, in his goodness, to bless them always!

In 1951, when Mother Ursula arrived at St Francis of Assisi Mission in Upi with Sisters Isabel, Helena, and Anita, I did not know that my life and that of my family would ever be so closely linked with theirs. I was in high school then. By the time I graduated from St Andrew's Seminary in Manila, in 1960, two novices had arrived —Sister Gloriana and Sister Theodora. I was assigned to assist Fr Charles Dunlap at the parish of St Francis. It was during that time that Sister Ana Clara and Sister Maria Agnes joined the Order. In 1968 Sister Maria Teresa arrived, and six years later, when I was visiting the convent in Arlington, I was blessed to be asked to officiate at her profession of life vows.

The Sisters made a tremendous contribution to the spiritual, social, and economic life of the great community of the parish in Upi, and in neighboring places near and far. Sister Isabel had charge of the girls in the school dormitory, and since she was a nurse as well, she assisted in the mission clinic. Besides taking care of business at the convent, Mother Ursula helped with church work and joined Sister Anita in the church school. It was Sister Anita who, with others, including Sister Helena and Sister Maria Agnes, started the embroidery room at the convent. They fashioned beautiful vestments, doing the exquisite embroidery by hand. Several women from the mission helped them, making it possible to earn some money. Recently this ministry has been revived, thanks to Sister Maria Agnes's cousin Teresita Capin Manguramas, with the encouragement of my wife, Esther Manguramas.

In time the convent in Upi became a branch house of the Order of Saint Anne. The four Sisters who had come in 1951 returned to the mother house, and Mother Miriam sent three Sisters from Arlington. One of them was Sister Olga, who is the godmother of our daughter Karla. In addition to other responsibilities, the Sisters went to teach at St Francis High School. Esther still remembers how the girls in the dormitory loved to watch the Sisters walk from the convent to the church—especially the beautiful sound of rosary beads.

Esther has been a dear friend of the Sisters since she was in high school, and we are both Associates of the Order—though I did not receive my Associate's medal until I had the wonderful opportunity to celebrate the Eucharist at the chapel in Arlington. We thank you, dear Sisters, for sharing your lives with us and with so many others. Your example of prayer and service makes God known to all the earth. God bless you all!

✠ Constancio B. Manguramas,
Bishop of Southern Philippines, retired

though silent
speak

14 Mission Far and Wide

Most of the work of the Order of Saint Anne will never be known except to God, for whose sake it has been carried out. Now and then a Sister with a penchant for writing has left a first-hand account of her community's life, its ministry, and occasionally its adventures. Some convents have had their historians, official and unofficial. For other times and places, information is less plentiful, but even so it confirms the verses published in GEMS when the Order marked its thirtieth anniversary:

> From out the heights of Arlington
> From slopes of Beacon Hill
> They spread all o'er the U.S.A.,
> And even farther still.
> So England, mother country, and
> The shores of far Cathay
> All know the well-worn habit
> Of the Sisters garbed in grey.
> For children, well and suffering,
> With skins of varying hue,
> Saint Anne's devoted daughters all
> Have works of love to do.

In 1919, for example, three years after the 'China Sisters' left for 'far Cathay,' the Order began a mission of 'rescue and prevention' for girls, near Christchurch in **New Zealand**, at the invitation of Archbishop Churchill Julius. The aim was to provide a cheerful

OPPOSITE: 'Though Silent I Speak'

Christian home, rather than a penitentiary. After four years, the work was handed over to a diocesan community, the Sisters of the Sacred Name, and the Saint Anne's Sisters came home to Arlington. But in 1974 the Order received a letter from the priest of what had in the meantime become a flourishing parish, thanking them in particular for the Sunday School they had started more than fifty years before.

From 1921 to 1930, Saint Anne's Sisters worked at St Thomas in the **Virgin Islands**. Their convent was attached to All Saints Church, one of the Anglican parishes that came into the Episcopal Church when the United States bought the islands from Denmark. A new mission district was formed, with the Bishop of Puerto Rico in charge, and at his urgent invitation 'a little company was set apart in the convent of St Anne's House, Boston, and having elected a Mother, they set forth to live and work among Christ's poor in the West Indies.' The parish they were assigned to was a big one, with nine hundred children in the Sunday School and three kindergartens. The Sisters taught in relays, with three

SMALLNESS

That the Houses of the Order of S. Anne shall be always small is in the very forefront of the Rule of the Order. Our families are never so distended in size as to lose the character of families. Family life develops individuality, which institutions tend to repress.
GEMS, February 1919

Mission Far and Wide 83

classes in the morning after solemn high Mass at eight, and two more before Evensong. On Saturdays and weekday afternoons, there were meetings of various parish guilds—sewing, music, drama, arts and crafts. For one Sister, Holy Innocents' Day was especially memorable. Mothers brought their babies to be blessed, 'about three hundred of them, row after row.'

Sisters from both the Arlington house of the Order and the Boston house founded a convent at **Kingston**, New York in 1925. Their ministry there is part of a larger story, which is told in a later chapter.

In **Denver** the Sisters' work began in 1929. It was at first connected with a sanitarium and later with a convalescent home for children, which occupied an old farmhouse and some of its outbuildings. The Chapel of the Holy Cross was 'made, like Bethlehem, out of a stable.' In keeping with the Order's mission of caring for children in need, the Sisters provided education for young sufferers from polio. By 1950, medical advances were

THE ONEIDA MISSION

At first the land was wild and hard, but generous and bountiful, and always beautiful. The Oneidas came and settled here and built their church, and their missionaries lived and died with them through all the many years.

Soon we who read these words will have become part of the past, and our spirits, too, will move with the wind through the tall, old trees.

And TA LUH YA WA GU, 'He who holds the Blue Heaven,' will smile on us all and welcome us to a new life where the sorrow of parting is no more.

Written for the 150th anniversary of Holy Apostles Church, Mission to the Oneidas, 1972

Mother Irene, Superior of the Denver convent, with a class of children.

making such a ministry less urgent, so a more traditional independent school was opened, which is now St Anne's Episcopal School. Later in the same year that three Sisters left for Denver, three others left for **Memphis**, Tennessee, to begin a house of the Order there. Two years after that, yet another group was called to **Versailles**, Kentucky, where they took charge of Margaret Hall School, a diocesan boarding school for girls.

In **Oneida**, Wisconsin, the Order of Saint Anne worked with the Oneida Mission, the Episcopal Church's oldest mission to Native Americans. The Sisters of the Holy Nativity had to withdraw in 1946, and from then until 1962 St Anne's House provided the Mission School with teachers. During that time, the Sisters did social work in Oneida, calling on homes, advising, giving instruction in mental and physical hygiene, and sometimes providing first aid and nursing. Sister Augusta, who had learned the art of making lace while she was in a prison camp in the Philippines, taught it to some of the children.

Sisters Edith, Augusta, and Mabel with Fr Harold Goetz and the Oneida community's new van.

The Chapel of St Anne's-in-the-Hills, Denver.

The rhythm band at Oneida.

Mission Far and Wide 85

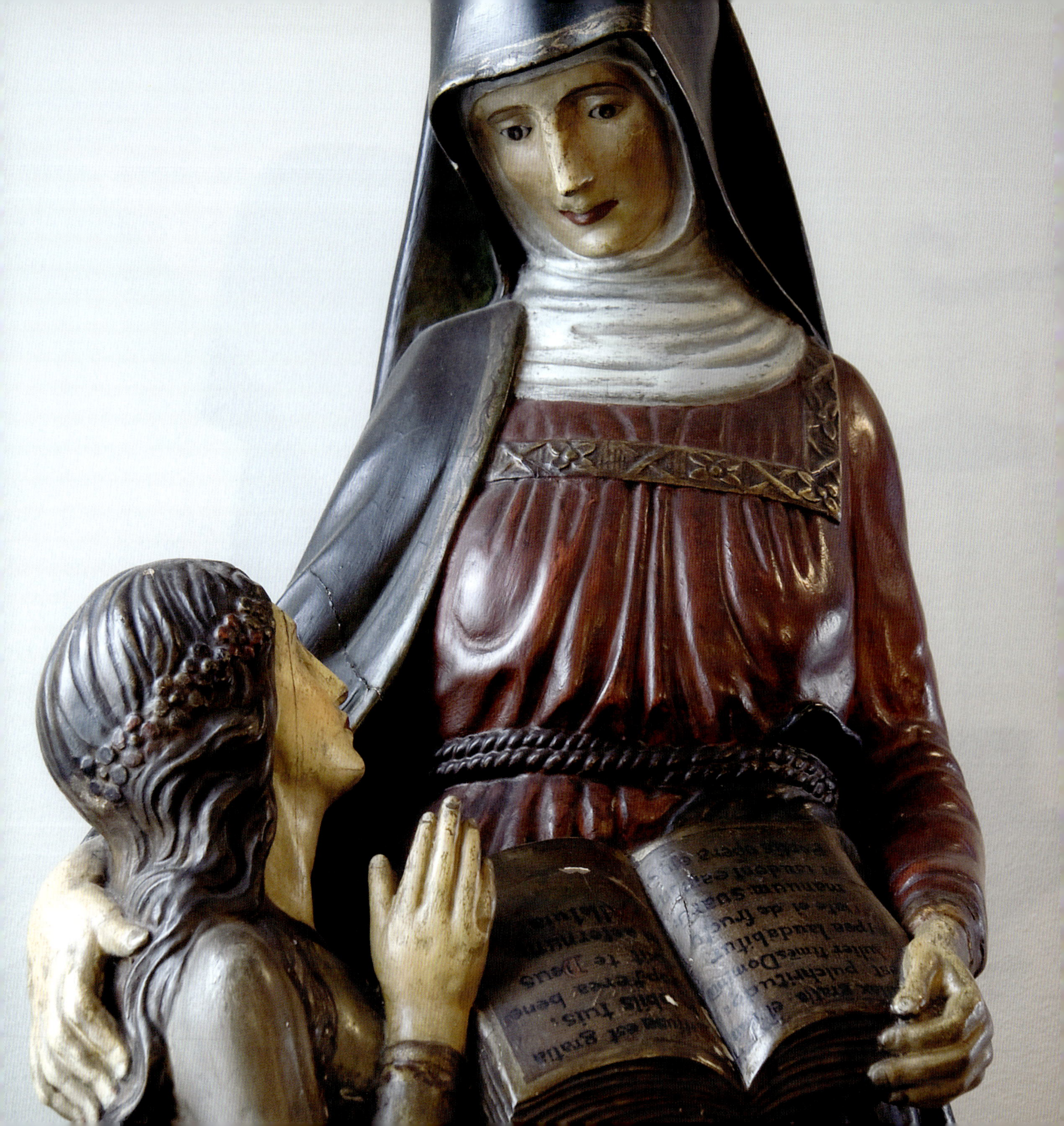

14 Chicago

The Chicago convent of the Order of Saint Anne began with an unexpected invitation. Just when four Sisters were about to leave for the Virgin Islands, a telegram arrived at St Anne's House, sent by two Sisters on their way home from North Dakota, announcing that they would not be returning just yet. The two had stopped in Chicago to change trains, and as they were waiting a priest from the Church of the Ascension had intercepted them to urge, earnestly and eloquently, that the place to found a convent was Chicago, not North Dakota, and that it should be founded then and there. Seizing the opportunity, the Sisters let the train leave without them.

When they did return to Boston, their report was favorable. Presently the invitation was accepted, and Sister Gabrielle was appointed as the first Superior. Shortly after being installed in the chapel at St Augustine's Farm in Foxborough, she left for Chicago. There, in June 1921, the Sisters of Saint Anne first took their places at the Church of the Ascension, in the front pew that has been theirs ever since. Later that summer, the parish vestry voted to renovate the second floor of the parish house as a residence. There the Sisters lived for eight years, using a chapel in the parish church for reciting the Daily Offices. The redoubtable Fr William Brewster Stoskopf, rector of Ascension, was their chaplain, and their many and various ministries were mainly connected with the parish. They took responsibility for teaching, altar work, visiting the sick, and preparing women and children for Holy Communion. One Sister served as parish secretary. Others did emergency nursing, and sometimes drove Fr Stoskopf to visit and administer Holy Communion to parishioners who were ill. On one such occasion, so the story is told, the Sister who was driving managed to violate a traffic regulation under the eye of a police officer, who waved the car to the side of the street. He was beginning to scold the embarrassed Sister when, from the back seat, Fr Stoskopf pointed out that she was acting as chauffeur for the Blessed Sacrament, whereupon the officer genuflected and waved them on.

Baking and selling altar bread helped towards making the convent self-supporting, and one of the Sisters took a job at Chicago's Newberry Library during and after the Depression of the 1930s. Meanwhile, the community had moved to a building of their own. Before they took it over, the new convent was described as a 'dirty old house,' but that soon changed. In 1944, Fr Stoskopf and his sister Alice paid off the mortgage as a memorial to their parents, for which a bronze tablet in the entry hall records the community's gratitude. Later Miss Stoskopf set up an endowment to support the Sisters for as long as they went on working in the parish of the Ascension, as they continue to do.

It was at their convent house, in 1932, that the Sisters began a small school for girls, among whom

OPPOSITE: St Anne teaching her daughter to read. The image stands in the Sisters' chapel at the convent in Chicago.

were a few boarders. Later a program in early childhood education was started. Many of the children in the preschool that opened in 1952 were from neighborhood families with no previous ties to the parish. State and city regulations made it necessary to transfer the preschool from the convent to the parish, but the Sisters continued to supply teachers and helpers. In 1963, the children in the class that had graduated (complete with cap and gown) from the kindergarten were keen to stay on, so the Sisters and the rector of the parish decided to start St Anne's School, which would later become the Ascension Parochial School. Mother Mary Margaret, who was the Superior for many years, served as the school's first principal. It was she who launched the project of remodeling the coach house at the back of the convent, which long served under the name of Bethlehem House as the center of the Sisters' ministry of hospitality.

Sister Augusta with her class at St Anne's School in Chicago

Preparing pumpkin pie for Thanksgiving dinner at the Church of the Ascension, Chicago.

Saint Anne's Sisters in Chicago: Sisters Mary Cecelia, Judith Marie (Superior), Barbara Louise, and Mary Margaret.

Interlude: Bethany Thanksgivings

In some very significant ways, the Bethany Sisters of the Order of Saint Anne raised me as a parish priest, notably and nobly suffering through the adolescence of my parochial vocation. When I arrived in Lincoln in 1986 and found that the convent was in my parish, I had no idea what a life-giving blessing that would turn out to be. I was a young, single, inexperienced, first-time rector, and these patient, prayerful, wise, and godly women took me in as a companion and friend. In the two decades that followed, they nurtured my faith and saw me through marrying, the births and adoptions of our children, and the many transitions and changes of my service to the church.

First in the bright, sun-splashed chapel of the convent on Sandy Pond Road, and then in the beautifully austere Cram chapel in Arlington, they listened to countless groggy-headed, early morning homilies, and then had the grace and generosity to feed me boiled eggs and loving care. Like the biblical garden from which they take their name, they provided a quiet and secure space for me to listen for God when I needed to most. They nourished me with their meals and nurtured me with their prayers, and no matter what the situation, they were patiently encouraging, gently extending an acceptance that reflects the heart of God.

Sister Olga's firm and frank companionship—first as Superior during times of great transition for her community, and later as colleague on the diocesan staff —and the deep affection with which God has blessed the two of us, have particularly sustained me through challenges of life and ministry. On my desk is a framed postcard of Rembrandt's *The Storm on the Sea of Galilee*, the masterpiece stolen from the Isabella Stewart Gardner Museum in 1990. Knowing of my fondness for this lost work of art, Sister Olga gave me the card years ago. It reminds me daily of her steadying presence in my life, no matter how stormy are the weather and waters through which I may sail.

And so it is deep, deep gratitude that fills my prayer as I contemplate a century of the ministry of the Order of Saint Anne, and especially the blessing of the Bethany Sisters. In their profound devotion, these women have taught me fidelity to God; in their ceaseless affection, they have taught me the fidelity of God.

✠ Mark Hollingsworth, Jr.
Eleventh Bishop of Ohio

Bishop Mark and Sister Olga

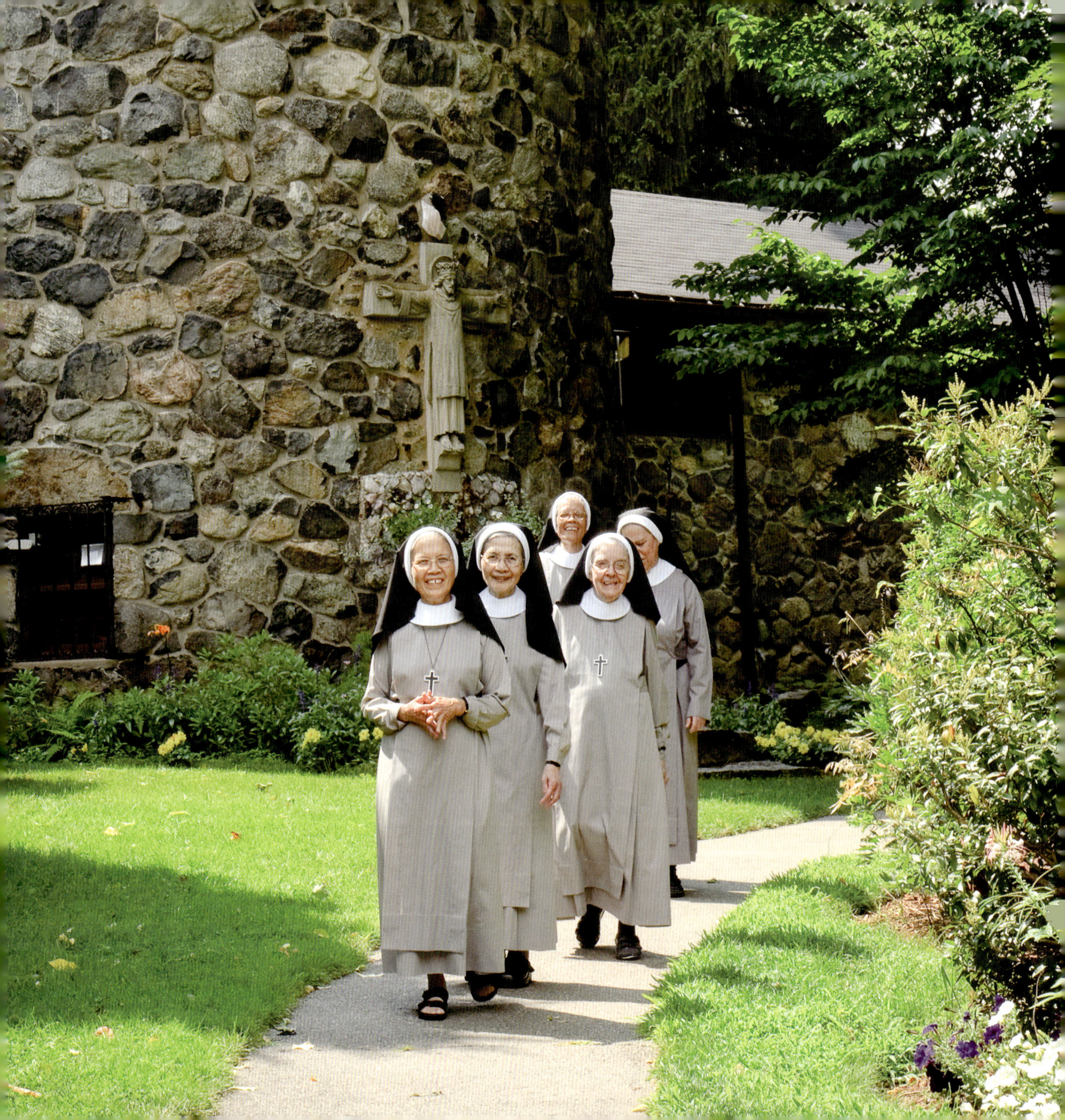

15 Bethany: Lincoln and Arlington

The newest convent of the Sisters of Saint Anne stands just a few yards from the first one. Here, on the same hillside where the Order began a hundred years ago, the heritage of its life and work in other places has been drawn together in a kind of homecoming.

One part of the story begins in Kingston, New York, where Sisters from both houses in Massachusetts founded a convent in 1925. The pattern that had unfolded in Arlington unfolded once again: a house was chosen, friends helped with their support, and by St Anne's Day the next year, five children were being cared for and the first novice had arrived. Legacies made it possible to convert a coach house into the House of the Holy Guardian Angels—'Angel House,' as it was called.

In time the Sisters shifted their ministry from children to older girls. Some of the teenagers who found a home with them at Kingston suffered from cerebral palsy; some had lasting brain injury; some were developmentally disabled. The Sisters not only lived among them but created together with them a community which was then without parallel in America. Did they know they were doing that? Perhaps not; but they found it out when, in the 1960s, the Order had to take a decision about continuing the work at Kingston. By then the buildings were outmoded and needed renovation. The convent itself was operating at a deficit, and the only prudent course, it seemed, was to close the whole operation. But as responses from the children's parents poured in, it became clear that closing would mean the loss of something uniquely valuable, indeed irreplaceable. The Order decided to reconsider.

The convent of the Order of Saint Anne at Kingston, New York.

Reconsidering involved consultations with universities and hospitals in and around Boston, and with the President's Committee on Mental Retardation in Washington. The result was a facility three times the size of the one at Kingston. Far from abandoning the ministry there, the Order expanded it. At first the project was called 'The Episcopal Church Center for Retarded Women,' but not for long. In the course of a discussion one evening in Arlington, someone mentioned Jesus' need to find a place where he could re-establish community. 'You know—like his trips to Bethany.' Soon it was as 'Bethany' that the new enterprise was going forward.

A site of thirty-one acres was found in Lincoln, a few miles from Arlington. Women of the Episcopal Church, through the United Thank Offering, made planning possible. For those who could make a thousand-dollar contribution, the 'Bethany Founders' was established, and Sister Germaine was determined to be first on the list. 'It wasn't long,' Fr Thomas Kershaw, the executive officer, reported, 'before every delivery man in Arlington knew about Bethany' and was reaching into his wallet so that Sister Germaine could be a Founder.

At its opening in 1971, the community at Bethany comprised the Sisters who had come from Kingston and the fourteen girls in their care, together with the Sisters from the convent in the Philippines, where political developments had made it advisable to relocate. The work that was beginning in Lincoln was symbolized by a statue outside the new building—a nun wearing the habit and cross of the Order of Saint Anne and sheltering a child as they both walk towards the door. Inside that door, Bethany's sunny, spacious design included bedrooms and dining rooms for the Sisters and the resident women, as well as a modern kitchen, a chapel and a library, a workshop for sewing and crafts, and facilities for exercise and entertainment. There was a residence for the administrator, Fr Frederick Bender, and his family. Later this was the home of Richard and Patricia Bennet, who between them devoted countless hours to the medical, financial, and personal well-being of the Bethany community. Also taking part in the Sisters' ministry were several lay staff members and scores of volunteers. Churches in the area helped with programs, and the residents themselves had various household jobs.

Growing Older

We give thanks for the courage and witness of our elderly Sisters and for the love and care of those who minister to them. The old have opportunities not given to others. Theirs is a God-given 'hour' to engage in the spiritual life at its deepest level. And we rejoice that heroic sanctity is found at unexpected times and unpromising places.
from 'We' magazine, summer 1982

All this made Bethany very different from the state institutions provided, at that time, for developmentally challenged people. The work the Order had undertaken was costly and labor-intensive, and as time went on the diminishment of their numbers and their energy raised the question of their ability to carry on their ministry among the 'Bethany ladies.' Small group homes, based in local communities, were becoming the norm, and the Sisters found they could no longer meet the requirements set by mental health authorities. After seventeen years in Lincoln, they made the decision to find a new home, carefully chosen, for each of the residents, and to return to Arlington.

It was a sad decision. The community was parting not only from a lovely home but from the women with whom they had shared it. And yet there were 'tears of joy,' as Sister Olga, the Superior then, would later put it—'joy for all we had together, joy for the advancement of our dear Bethany ladies, joy for all the great things that lay ahead for each of them, joy for our return to our founding convent in Arlington with its beautiful, wonderful chapel and garden, joy for our uniting again with our Sisters there, who welcomed us with love and anticipation.'

The altar in the chapel at Bethany in Lincoln.

An outdoor gathering at Bethany, Lincoln. The guitarists are Sister Ana Clara and Sister Deborah Anne.

Preparing altar bread at Bethany, Lincoln.

Sister Johanna with one of the 'Bethany ladies,' Johanna Gallop.

Bethany—Lincoln and Arlington 93

Sisters Ana Clara, Amy Inez, Olga,
and Maria Agnes breaking ground
for their new convent on Hillside Avenue in 1991.

The statue facing the door at Bethany, Lincoln.

The convent at 25 Hillside Avenue, Arlington.

94   Catch the Vision

In Arlington, the Bethany Sisters continued as a distinct community, and a new convent was built for them on Hillside Avene, to the east of St Anne's Chapel. It was a time for reflection on what was most important to the Sisters, now that they were fewer than they had been in Lincoln. In the course of much prayer and many conversations, they identified these essentials:

- a place to stay
- privacy for solitude and community life
- something to do: a ministry
- something to pray for: a sense of purpose and involvement
- community, among themselves and with the church and the world
- the Eucharist and the Divine Office
- a sense of beauty

As many of the reflections in this book testify, the Sisters have shared these central values with 'all sorts and conditions' of people, welcoming to the convent clergy and layfolk from the diocese, and providing hospitality for ministries such as the monthly training weekends for those who aspire to be ordained to the vocational diaconate.

Christian convents and monasteries have a way of gathering around them communities of mutual cooperation and inspiration. Sometimes these take the institutional shape of third or 'tertiary' orders, 'companions,' or 'associates,' but often they are informal, though no less important for that. The Bethany convent has been no exception. 'It is amazing,' Thomas Shaw, their Bishop Visitor, once said, 'that something so small can have such influence.' As times change, and with them the needs of the church and the world, new patterns of collegiality are being tried out. At Bethany the Sisters have had many proposals to ponder and many opportunities to weigh, as they discern the role they can most responsibly assume while maintaining the integrity of their religious vocation.

St John's House, home of the Bethany House of Prayer.

One seed that has grown and flourished was planted shortly after the new Bethany convent was finished. The Revd Tansy Chapman asked if she might have a place there to offer a ministry of spiritual direction. At first the answer was *no*, but after a while it changed to *yes*. In time she was joined by others—Mary Meader, Patricia Boyd, Julia Slayton. Little by little, with the Sister's help and trust in 'the slow work of God,' their ministry took shape and they became a community.

From these beginnings, still quietly and gradually, grew the Bethany House of Prayer, officially 'a ministry with the Order of Saint Anne.' The initial founders, together with Karen Bettacchi, constitute the aptly-named 'Alongsiders,' working alongside the Sisters, meeting with them, and coordinating an array of quiet days, retreats, and opportunities for spiritual direction, contemplation, and companionship. While neither they nor the other Colleagues in Ministry who are associated with BHOP are monastics, they have 'the extraordinary privilege,' as Julia Slayton, the current director, has put it, 'of having our everyday lives informed and transformed by living closely by women who have chosen to live out their faithfulness as Sisters of the Order of Saint Anne. They change us. Our proximity to the Sisters and their way of life opens us to God's generosity, in a way that perhaps is not unlike the experience of those early Christians who took up residence near the Desert Fathers and Mothers.'

If Mother Etheldred could visit 'the small house at Arlington' today, there would surely be much to surprise her. But surely too she would recognize—and be grateful for—a deep continuity of purpose, despite the passing of a hundred years.

The Library at 25 Hillside Avenue.

96 ᛞ Catch the Vision

The Refectory. Among the guests are postulants and candidates for the Vocational Diaconate in the Diocese of Massachusetts.

The Holy Spirit Chapel. The Blessed Sacrament is reserved in the freestanding aumbry at the east end. In the niche to the left the remains of the Father Founder are buried.

Young adults from the Diocese on retreat with the Bethany House of Prayer.

Interlude: Seasons of Love

Memory is a strange thing. The image that comes to mind when I think of my dozen years of friendship with the Bethany Sisters is of an intricately wrought mandala. Every thought I have of them draws me back to the center. There is a chronology of course. I am here now in California listening to the surf of the Pacific Ocean pound against the rocks. It is February and the temperature mild, daffodils in bloom. I picture the Sisters braving freezing temperatures making their way along the snowy path to Chapel. Icicles hang down over the window that used to be my office. Soon I will hear the bell rung for noontime prayer. In my memory, someone comes up the office steps, stamps the snow off his or her boots, and sits on the blue and white couch opposite. We begin with silence, hearing the high voices of the nuns singing their devotions.

Year in, year out, men and women, by some incredible grace, come seeking a companion on their spiritual journey—a happening made possible only by the encircling generosity, love, and prayer of the Sisters. The seasons change in the beautifully kept gardens: flowering trees in the spring, immaculate lawns for St Anne's Day in the summer, colored lights at Christmas.

Seasons were evident not only in the garden and the chapel, but inside the convent too. More and more the Sisters shared the beauty of their home with all who came to the door. Groups were welcomed, as were individuals seeking a place to grieve, to heal. There were illnesses, partings, deaths, as the community dwindled. Gifts of flowers arrived for birthdays, anniversaries, Valentine's Day, Mother's Day—every plant and bouquet an expression of genuine love by Associates and friends. I learned so much from this tiny group of women about hospitality, and will remember always the cries of delight when a guest arrived regardless of

98 ଽ Catch the Vision

how tired they must sometimes have been feeling.

When the retreat house, St John's, first opened in 1995 the Sisters and I sprinkled the rooms with holy water, consecrating space that had once housed girls from the Order's school. Colleagues told me I should print up brochures, start programs. These things would come, but not then, not for many years. First, I learned from the Sisters, we wait and we pray for what will be revealed in God's time. Meanwhile directees arrived doubtful, depressed, searching. The Sisters prayed for them, invited them to the Eucharist, fed them breakfast, and above all, loved them. Lives changed in an atmosphere of complete, non-judging acceptance.

Mary Meader came—such a delight to have a soul sister. We started a group. The Sisters invited us in to reflect on their own discernment as they bravely faced the reality that the Order of Saint Anne was slowly diminishing. Ideas were discussed. Mary's gifts helped all of us see that all along a new ministry was being born.

Pat Boyd and Julia Slayton joined Mary and me, and were officially named the 'Alongsiders.' We met regularly by ourselves and with the Sisters, forming close bonds that came out of developing trust that God had brought us together. Between us we Alongsiders lived through various dramas in our own lives: pregnancy, birth, death, illness, divorce. I am ever grateful to Mary, Pat, and Julia for their creativity, faith, and friendship. I can only imagine the courage it took for the Bethany Sisters to open their lives to us. The retreat house, newly named Bethany House of Prayer, blossomed under the inspired leadership of Julia. I liked to refer to it as B-HOP. The work continues there and so do the Sisters, supported by an endless network of friends from near and afar.

The Revd Tansy Chapman

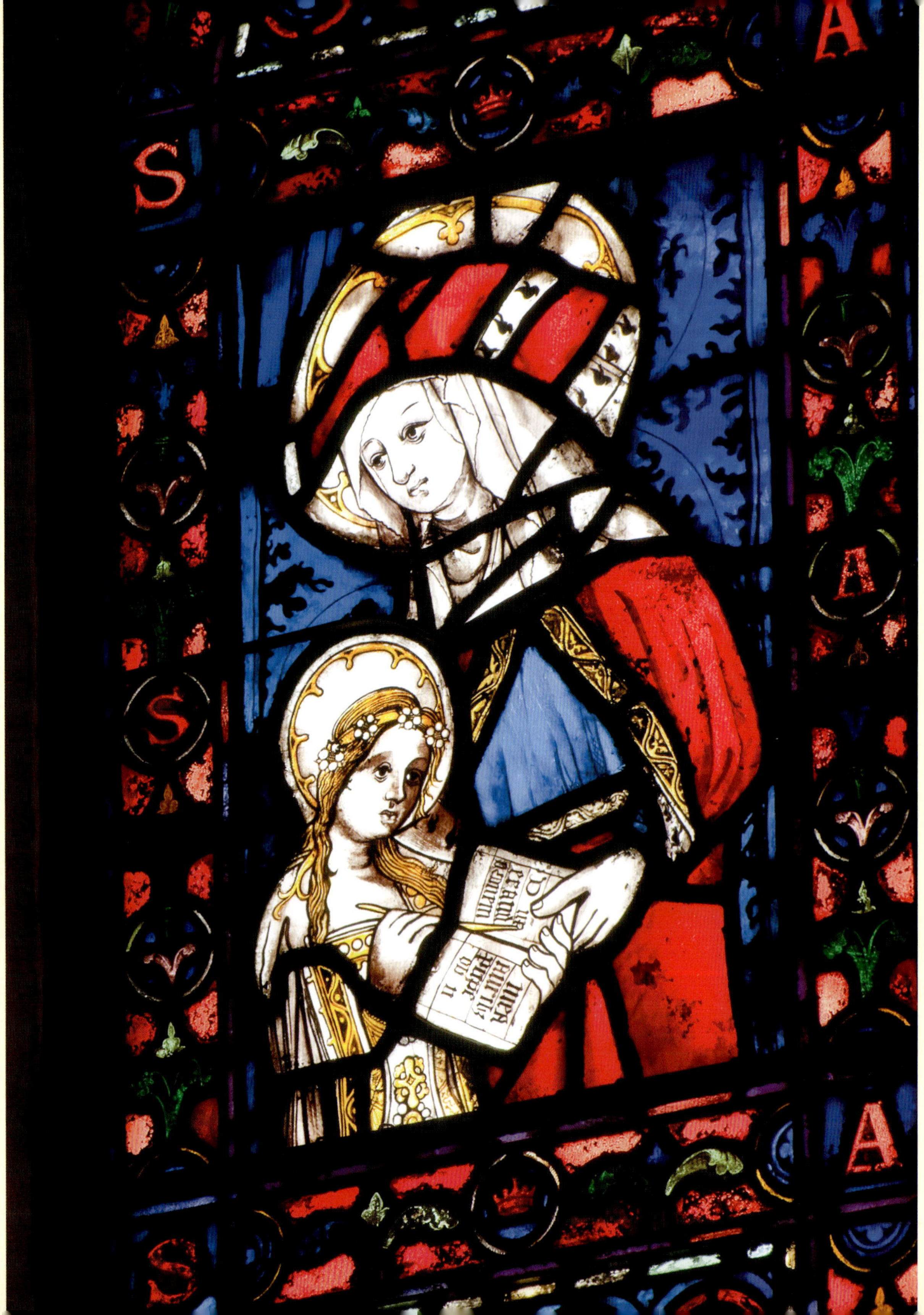

Postlude: Reading the Word

Sometimes a certain constellation of events and people comes together at a particular moment to set in motion something unique and needed in our world. So it was, more than a century ago, at 181 Appleton Street in Arlington. Two lives, Etheldred Breeze Barry and Frederick Cecil Powell, SSJE encountered one another and there began an adventure in the life of the Spirit that is still being written today.

As reflected throughout this book, the Sisters of Saint Anne have cultivated a heart of hospitality and gratitude that is without compare. Today, the five Sisters at the Bethany Convent will stop what they are doing the moment someone crosses their threshold, especially if it is a child. In their delight and gentleness, their humor and compassion, we can almost glimpse those with whom they have lived and ministered. They have let themselves be formed and changed by serving grace in the other.

Essential to the still unfolding story of the Order of Saint Anne is the Sisters' ultimate trust in the centrality of God's love and their complete offering of themselves to God's desire for them. Countless times, they have been undaunted by realities that to many would have seemed obstacles—finding themselves without the finances to cover their costs, or without a place to stay or to carry out a ministry. In their prayers, they have asked for what was needed, have rejoiced in what they had, and have been unafraid to invite others to be creative with them. Often, especially in their early years, they set out like Abraham and Sarah, creating homes for others and entertaining angels unawares, while seeking themselves to live without attachment to any one place.

As their numbers diminish, the Sisters continue to do what they have always done. They listen, pray, talk, wait, discern, and remain open to new invitations. In so doing, they offer their presence and the spaciousness of years of prayer to all those in need of such grounding and love.

To the same hillside from which the Sisters of Saint Anne set out so many times, they have returned. There, in the beautiful simplicity of their stone chapel, a stained glass window tells their story well. It shows St Anne holding a book open for her daughter Mary as she reads. It is an image of what our beloved Sisters of Saint Anne have been teaching us—how to live and understand and draw near to the very word of God that is being written with each of our lives. May we, like them and with them, be astonished and full of thanksgiving for the mystery and grace of God in the Word made flesh among us.

Julia Slayton
Executive Director,
The Bethany House of Prayer

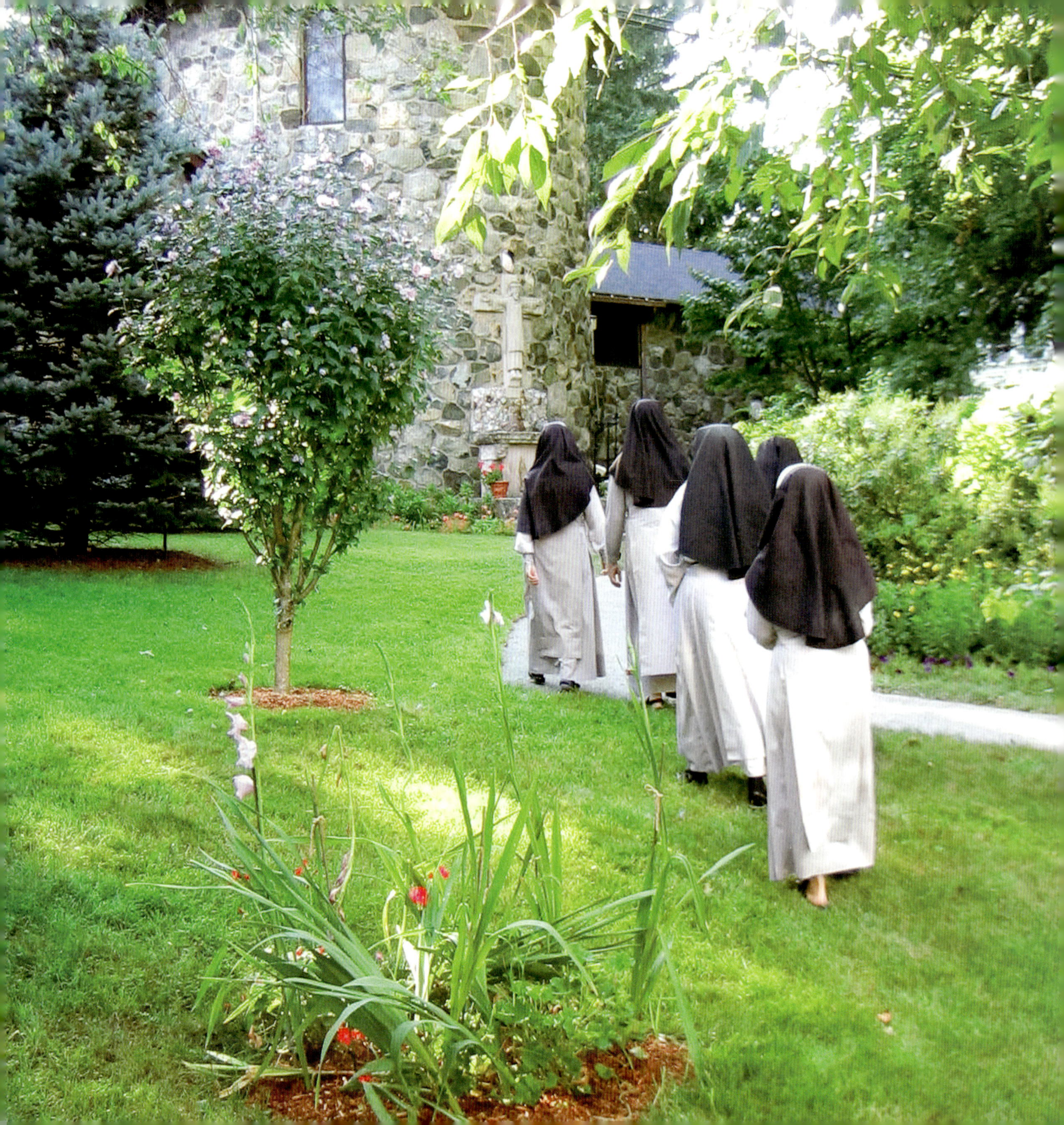

Envoi: There's So Much More

I read once about a Palestinian youth who said: 'All my life I have dreamed of seeing my village once again.' Within each of us, I believe, is this village, this personal paradise, this remembrance of times and places and dear persons from our past. That nostalgia never, ever leaves us. Then, sometimes, a special occasion comes our way and we are asked for 'a memory or two' in order to show our love for loved ones and dear days and dear places—and suddenly, it isn't too hard to return in mind and spirit to those dear ones and places.

I cannot pretend that I know what stirred in the heart of our Mother Foundress, Sister Etheldred Breeze Barry, an artist and a poet and one who envisioned in heart and mind our beloved OSA. I do know and believe wholeheartedly that she felt moved by God's love and God's vision of a religious order, drawing her to the Founding of the Order of Saint Anne.

Now here we are, a hundred years later. We Sisters in Arlington ought to take pleasure in our past, in our former OSA Mothers and Sisters, who are not behind us. They are ahead of us, urging us not to look back to where we imagine they may still be, but to run forward and catch them waving us on. We ought to relish imagining them as they call out to us: 'There's more, there's more, there's so much more.' I cannot imagine that those early women were completely prepared, equipped, competent! I just think they were in love. We five Sisters here and our four Sisters in Chicago love our past history, even as we seek God's way with our present and our future. We need our friends, relations, and Associates to pray that we may keep in mind and heart the words of our Father Founder, Frederick Cecil Powell, SSJE. In 1914 he said to our Sisters: 'What a name for a religious house—Bethany—the retreat of our Saviour, the home of the wearied Christ.'

In this twenty-first-century world of shadows and fears, of hesitation to follow a dream, some things are luminously clear: a call from God, who knows who each of us is whom he calls, and whose enthusiasm for what we are and what we can become is surely his greatest joy and hope.

Sister Olga, OSA

Launch Out

There would be fewer disappointments and lost vocations if we remembered that the Religious Life is only romantic when we look forward to it or look back to it. It is the ship on the horizon that is romantic. To those on board there may be drudgery. The command to us is: 'Launch out into the deep.'

F. C. Powell, SSJE,
in 'A Guide Book, or Microcosmographia Religiosa,' 1923

OF YOUR CHARITY PRAY FOR THE SOUL OF
FRANCES BARRY Dec·VIII·MCM·

Thank you

> Yea, a joyful and pleasant thing it is
> to be thankful.
> PSALM 147

Acknowledgments

The making of this book has been helped by many friends in many ways. Thanks are due first of all to the writers of the Interludes, and with them those whose written contributions informed several chapters, especially Gunesh Gery, Edward C. Lawrence, Sister Judith, OSA, and Richard Bennett.

In addition to the Sisters of Saint Anne themselves, all manner of folk have been generous with their expert knowledge, reminiscences, and advice—alumnae of St Anne's School; the late G. Barry McMennamin, nephew of Mother Etheldred; Marilyn Justice of the Connick Stained Glass Foundation; and at the Diocese of Massachusetts Tracy Sukraw, editor of *Episcopal Times*, and Lynn Smith, Diocesan Registrar-Historiographer.

The chapters on Foxborough and on the Father Founder draw in various ways on the longstanding friendship between the Order of Saint Anne and the Society of Saint John the Evangelist—Curtis Almquist, SSJE and Eldridge Pendleton, SSJE in particular.

For guidance and help with photography in the chapter on the Chicago convent, we are grateful to Charles M. Taylor, Director of Finance and Administration at The Church of the Ascension, Suzanne M. Lenz, and Scott Smith.

The artistry, patience, and tireless attention to detail that Claire MacMaster and Gregory Wostrel brought to the book can be seen from cover to cover. Words sufficient to express our gratitude are hard to find.

Sources

Especially for its account of the early years of the Order of Saint Anne, this book has drawn mainly on these sources:

The Order of St. Anne—It's First Foundation, a volume of recollections written by Mother Etheldred, OSA for her Sisters in the Order. There are two nearly identical copies in her own hand, neither of which is dated. Though not intended for publication, much of the manuscript is accurately transcribed in *A Theme for Four Voices*, listed on 107.

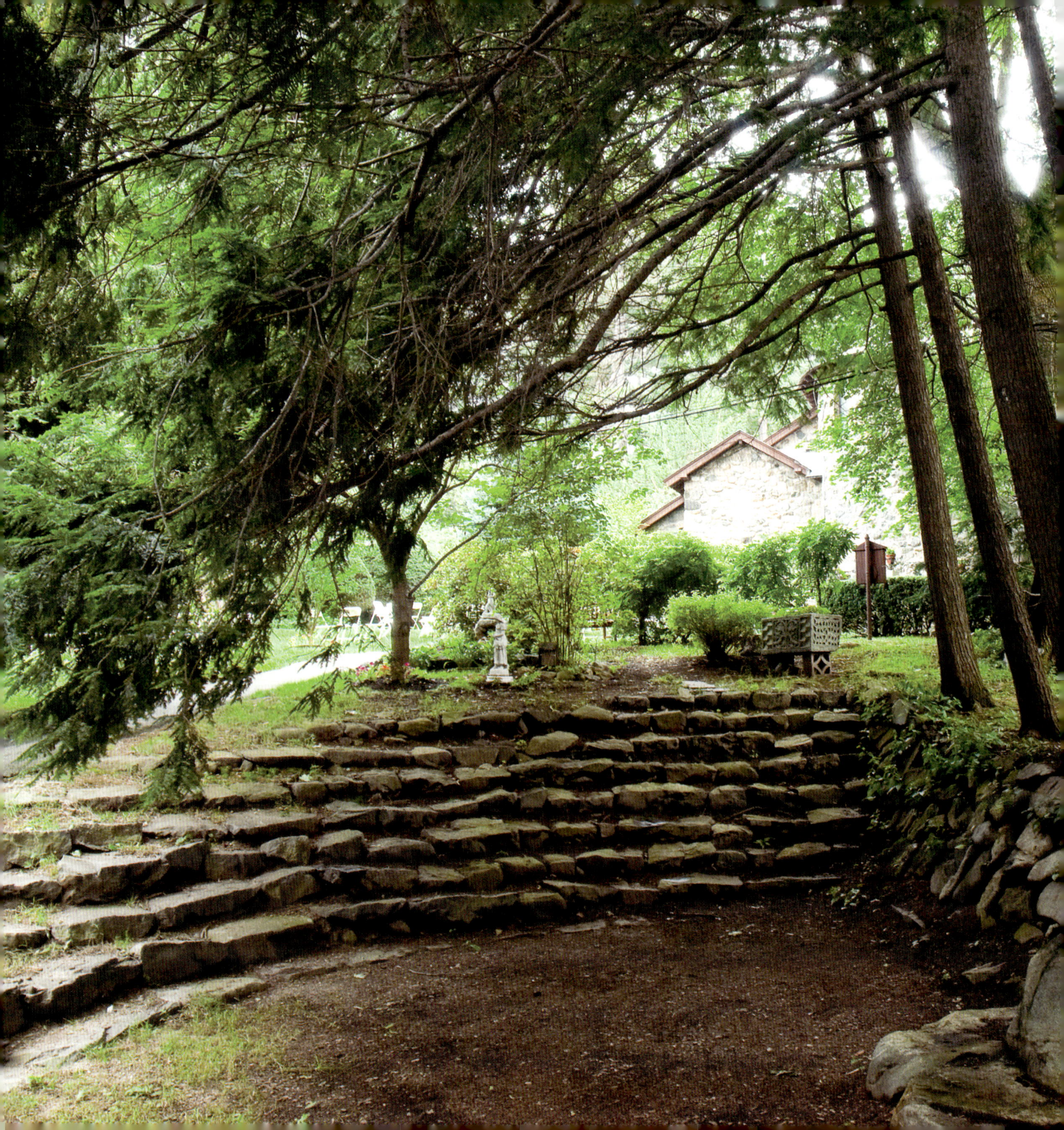

A Guide Book or Microcosmographia Religiosa: Describing the Life and Work of St. John's House Arlington Heights, Massachusetts and Other Convents of The Order of S. Anne. This book, which was published in 1923 at St Anne's House, 44 Temple Street, Boston, does not name an author, but both the prose style and later references make it all but certain that F. C. Powell, SSJE wrote the greater part of the text, if not the whole.

The Reverend Frederick Cecil Powell, SSJE, an unpublished biography of the Father Founder by Constance Grosvenor Alexander. Completed around 1945, it quotes extensively from Fr Powell's letters. The typescript, with some corrections by a later hand, is in the archives of the Society of Saint John the Evangelist in Cambridge.

A New Fairy Tale: Being a Little Account of the Founding & Works of the Order of St. Anne 1910–1960. This booklet of 34 pages, printed at Kingston, New York around 1960, highlights the founding of the convent in Kingston.

My Fifty Years in the Convent (1926-1976), a booklet of reminiscences by Sister Augusta Mary, OSA, was 'published under the Auspices of the diocese of Eastern Massachusetts of the Episcopal Church in the United States of America,' presumably not long after 1976.

A Theme for Four Voices, edited by Sister Johanna, OSA was printed for the seventy-fifth anniversary of the Order in 1985. In addition to transcribing Mother Etheldred's narrative, Sister Johanna made use of an account (no longer extant) of the beginnings of St Anne's House in Boston and the Second Order Sisters, written by Sister Felicia Anne. A letter written by Christopher McFadden is also included.

GEMS, published (and for a time printed) by the Order of Saint Anne, was issued monthly from 1910 to 1932, and then four times a year until around 1967.

Other archival sources, located at the convent in Arlington, include *We*, an occasional newsletter issued by the Bethany community at Lincoln in the 1970s and 1980s; letters written by Mother Ursula, OSA, to the Sisters in Arlington and to her mother, Mrs Alden, from 1916 on; a brief autobiographical account written by Sister Helena, OSA; and letters from Mother Miriam, OSA, and other Superiors of the Order.

Research in the Order's archives and elsewhere was undertaken by Dr Erica Gelser.

The numbered chapters were written by Prof Charles Hefling.

MCMXIV — MCMXVIII

Picture Credits

The scrolls and borders that appear at the beginning of chapters and elsewhere are details from illuminated manuscripts and drawings of Mother Etheldred, OSA. The watercolor sketches of the Emsworth convent on pages 66 and 69 may also be her work, but the attribution is not certain.

Many of the photographs are reproduced from material in the archives of the Order, housed at the convent in Arlington. Credits for original photography follow.

Gregory Wostrel, gwcreative.com:
  pages 4, 6-7, 8, 10, 12, 13, 22, 26, 31, 35 (right), 38, 41, 42, 45 (both), 46 (background), 48, 52, 54, 55, 56, 59 (both), 60, 61, 63 (bottom), 65, 69 (upper right), 70, 75, 76, 82, 90, 94 (lower left), 95, 96, 97 (upper left and upper right), 100, 104, 106, 108

Julia Slayton, Bethany House of Prayer:
  pages 28 (lower left), 31 (bottom), 46 (center), 89, 97 (bottom), 99, 102

Scott Smith, S Smith Photography:
  pages 86, 88 (lower left)

Susie White:
  page 98

Courtesy of *Episcopal Times*, Diocese of Massachusetts:
  pages 11, 94 (upper left)

Courtesy of the Society of Saint John the Evangelist
  pages 43, 58 (both)

The diagram on pages 110–111, showing the lineage of the various convents of the Order of Saint Anne, is the work of Rob Leanna.

1910

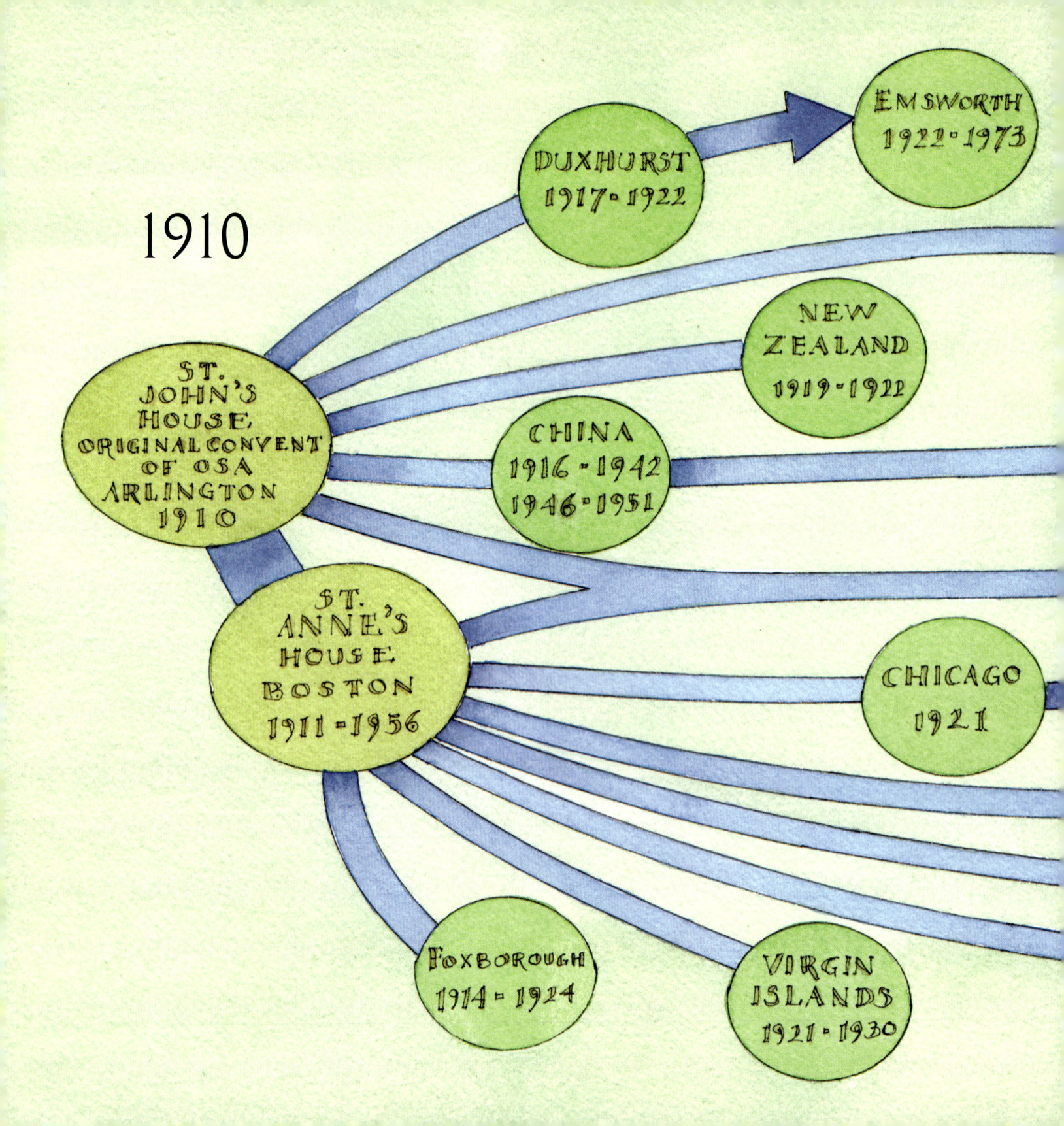

Houses of the Order of Saint Anne

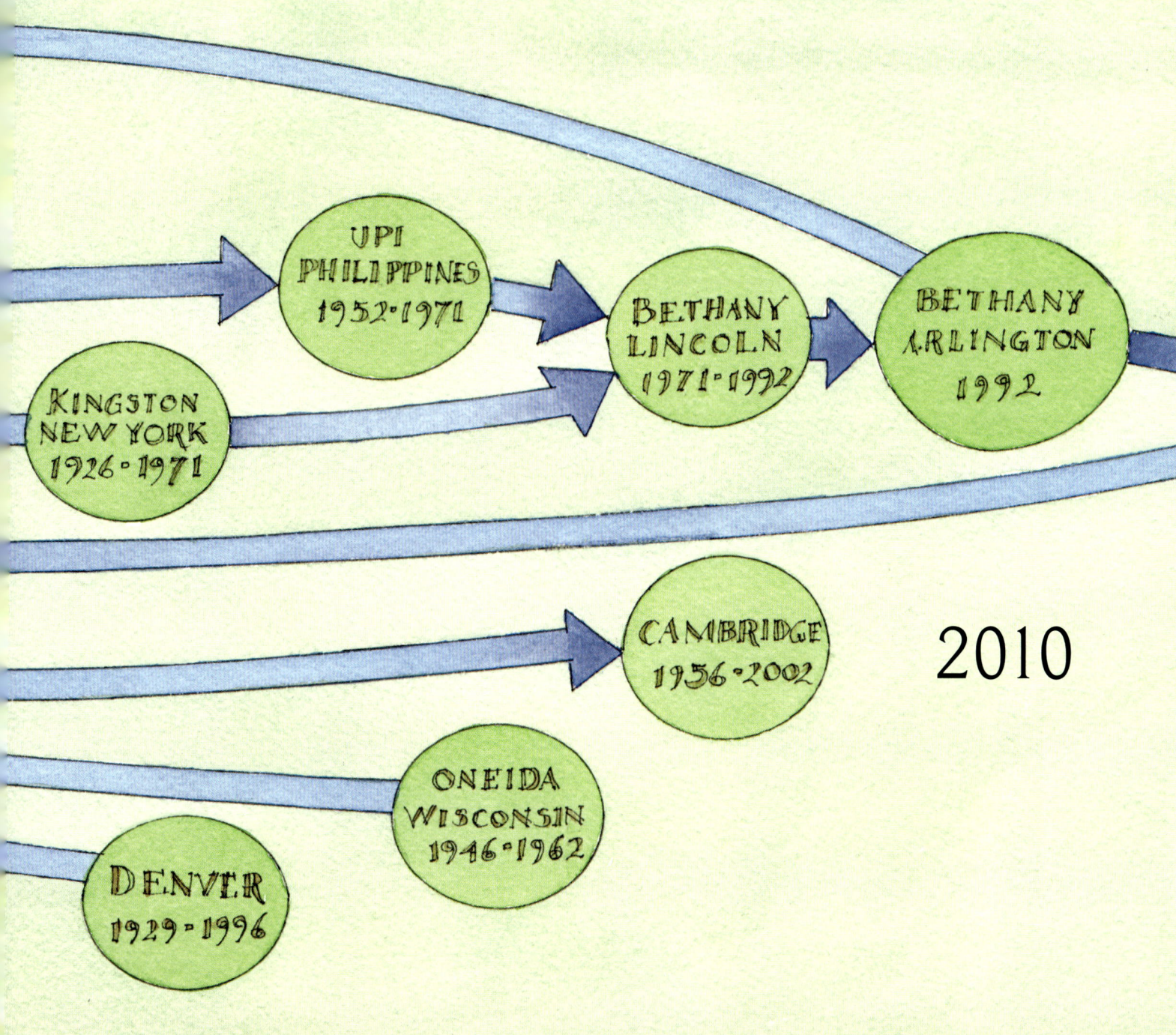

2010

- Kingston New York 1926-1971
- UPI Philippines 1952-1971
- Bethany Lincoln 1971-1992
- Bethany Arlington 1992
- Cambridge 1956-2002
- Oneida Wisconsin 1946-1962
- Denver 1929-1996

In Gratitude

This book could not have been written without the gifts of Charles Hefling who with eloquent precision, patience, breadth of knowledge and love of the church, has rendered to all the story of the Sisters of St. Anne with charity and beauty. We are forever grateful to Charles for offering his gifts to the telling of our adventure in the life of the Spirit.

The Sisters of the Order of St. Anne-Bethany
and the Editorial Working Group